Soap and Scent

Soap and Scent:

Making Organic Cosmetics for Natural Beauty

GILL FARRER-HALLS

Published in the UK in 2004 by
Apple Press
Sheridan House
112-116A Western Road
Hove BN3 1DD
UK

www.apple-press.com

ISBN 1-84092-472-1

10 9 8 7 6 5 4 3 2 1

Design: Toby Matthews, toby.matthews@ntlworld.com
Photography: Robin Bath
Book packaged by Angie Patchell, atpatchell@ntlworld.com

Printed in China

Contents

Introduction

"I commend to you organically grown essential oils and herbs, wild crafted and harvested materials as the beautiful bounty of nature."
—Jan Kusmirek, aromatherapist, medical herbalist, and naturopath

Introduction
the organic philosophy

Looking back over the last couple of decades, it is clear that increasing numbers of people have developed the desire for a more natural lifestyle. They have also realized the importance of an ethical responsibility and a considerate attitude toward the environment. These two concerns are united in the philosophy of organics. As part of the Green Movement, organics is seen as a positive counter force to the excessive use of chemicals in all aspects of our lives.

On hearing the word organic, most people usually think first of organic vegetables, fruits, and other natural foods, and then of how these foods are grown and produced. This in turn harks back to the traditional methods of local subsistence farming. This natural farming was practiced successfully until population growth and urbanization created a demand for large quantities of food to feed the populations of huge cities. Intensive farming methods were soon developed, and alongside the introduction of battery farms and massive farm machinery came the use of agrochemicals.

Unfortunately, the use of agrochemicals such as herbicides, pesticides, and chemical fertilizers can cause long-term damage to the countryside and the birds and animals that inhabit it. Crops grown with agrochemicals do not taste as good, nor are they as full of natural goodness, as their organic counterparts. So, not only does organic agriculture mean growing natural produce without pesticides and herbicides but also ensuring that the environment is sustained healthily, and neither animals nor the countryside are exploited.

We are more than what we eat, however, and the organics philosophy can be extended beyond farming and food production into all other areas of life. We can respect ourselves and our whole environment by using natural, organic products wherever and whenever possible. Several companies manufacture biodegradable washing and cleaning products that do not pollute the environment. We can reuse plastic bags and compost our vegetable trimmings and leftover foods to minimize landfill sites. We can also recycle glass, paper, and aluminum cans; use natural, organic cosmetics; and wear clothes made of natural fibers.

In this spirit, *How to Make Your Own Organic Cosmetics: Soap and Scent* introduces the idea of making soaps and scents using natural, organic ingredients. Making your own soap is not a new idea. In centuries past if you didn't manufacture some sort of basic soap or cleanser yourself, then you simply went without, because there was no commercially produced soap. These early forms of soap were made from natural ingredients. These included animal fats, clays, ashes, and plant material from herbs such as soapwort, which—as the name implies—gives a slippery, soapy lather with cleansing properties similar to, but less efficient than, modern-day soap.

The recipes in this book have come a long way forward since these early soap recipes, and the soaps are much more sophisticated than the early forms of soap described above. One of the major differences between the two types of soap is the addition of perfume. The recipes here suggest using only plant-based, natural scents in the form of essential oils. Essential oils have been used for thousands of years, not only for their wonderful perfuming qualities, but also for their health and beauty properties. Choosing the essential oils you wish to use in your soaps is, therefore, an art, in which you balance the fragrance and properties to suit your individual taste and requirements.

While the early soaps were utilitarian, and designed only for removing as much grime as possible, the soaps we make and use today are sweet smelling, and designed to make washing a pleasant and enjoyable experience, not just a necessary function. Interestingly, the 16th century British Queen Elizabeth, alongside many of her subjects, was reputed to take only one bath a year as any more was considered injurious to health! Our modern daily bathing rituals are considerably more hygienic, and enhanced both by modern plumbing and the abundant varieties of soap available to us today.

Once the idea of aesthetic appreciation and enjoyment of using soap is entertained, then a whole world of difference opens up. No longer do we choose soap just for its cleansing properties, but for a whole host of other a reasons. This means we look carefully at all the different ingredients that went into making the soap we use, to see how these may be of benefit to our skin and general health and well being. For example, once you know that honey nourishes the skin and is a natural moisturizer and that oatmeal softens the skin and is a natural exfoliator, then you can choose a traditional oatmeal and honey soap if it suits your skin type.

The book offers suggestions and ideas on making soaps that are natural and in harmony with nature and our own bodies. Many products and ingredients in the book can be sourced from organic suppliers, and the recipes suggest using only vegetable and mineral ingredients that are not tested on animals. Although obviously not designed for internal consumption, these soaps and scents are literally good enough to eat. Making and using these natural, organic soaps and scents is not only fun, imaginative, and creative, but good for you, mind, body, and spirit, and of benefit to the whole environment.

1 All About Soap

All About Soap

The quotation on page 17 describes briefly the science of soap, or in other words, how and why soap cleans. You will also discover from the quote that soap is made primarily from fat or oil and caustic soda, which doesn't make soap sound very nice! That is why this book suggests ways of making soaps that are kind to your skin and the environment. By using pure vegetable oils and plant-based colors, essential oils, and other organic nutrients, you can create soaps that look and feel close to nature.

Soap has an interesting history, and according to legend was discovered by accident in ancient Rome. To please their gods, the Romans performed animal sacrifices on Sapo Hill. The women rinsed their clothes in the Tiber River, which runs at the base of Sapo Hill. The women noticed a soapy mix of animal fat and caustic wood ashes seeping into the river. When this came in to contact with their clothes, the dirt on them seemed to magically wash away. After this discovery, soap was made deliberately and proved most popular.

European's interest in washing declined after the fall of the Roman Empire. However, in the seventh century, soap was produced again in limited quantities in Italy, France, and Spain, but only as a luxury item for the wealthy. Therefore, making basic soap at home, from scraps of animal fat, became part of the seasonal cycle of village life.

Early forms of soap were made using animal fat. Today's commercially produced soap is still made with tallow, although all-vegetable soaps are becoming increasingly available. In keeping with the organic ethics of this book, all the included recipes use only vegetable oils.

Animal fats are highly saturated and clog the skin's pores, causing blackheads and other blemishes. Tallow can also cause eczema and allergies in people with sensitive skin. Animal fats are used in soap production however because they are considerably cheaper and easier to use, as they can withstand higher temperatures and are less temperamental than vegetable oils.

Health-food shops and herbal gift shops offer pure, organic, all-vegetable soaps, which, although lovely to use and ethically produced, are quite expensive. When you make your own soap, you use only quality ingredients that are suited to your skin. And after the initial outlay of purchasing basic soap making ingredients, you might even find you'll be saving money on soap.

"Soap is a chemical combination of caustic soda and fat or oil. The soap molecule has two ends. One end—the caustic soda—is attracted to water. The other end—the fat or oil—is attracted to grease and dirt. Thus, although they normally don't mix, the soap pulls grease and dirt into solution in water."
  —Ian Marshall, doctor, psychotherapist & author

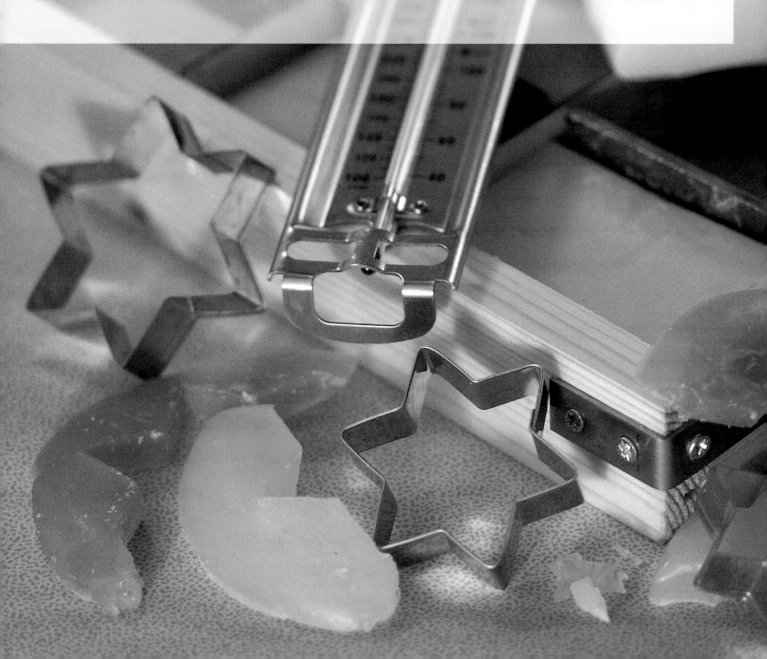

Did You Know? The German chemist Justus von Leibig suggested that much could be learned about a nation by measuring its per capita consumption of soap. Accordingly, those countries that used the most soap were the most civilized.

What You Will Need

Most basic soap making equipment can be found in the kitchen, so you probably don't have to buy a lot of extra implements. Make sure you wash all kitchen utensils thoroughly after making soap before using them again for cooking. You will need the following utensils:

- Scales, preferably digital and electronic. Weighing ingredients, even liquids, is more accurate than measuring by volume. Accurate measuring of ingredients—especially for cold-process soaps—is crucial.
- A large, stainless-steel or ceramic saucepan or pot, which is resistant to corrosion from lye, the solution of caustic soda and water. A double boiler is also necessary for some recipes.
- A large, lye-resistant glass bowl
- A cheese grater
- A sharp knife
- A large glass measuring cup and a smaller measuring cup
- An electric beater or hand whisk
- A cooking thermometer
- Rubber gloves and protective eye glasses or goggles—caustic soda and lye can cause nasty burns if they touch the skin, so they must be treated carefully and with respect. Wear the gloves and goggles throughout the entire process when you make cold-process soap.
- A wooden or stainless-steel spoon
- A mortar and pestle
- Soap molds—specially designed soap molds; cookie, jello, or cake molds; small cups and bowls; or even small cardboard boxes. Most recipes make approximately twelve bars of soap in a professional soap mold. If you use jello molds, cups, bowls, etc, then estimate the size of each mold according to a bar of soap, and prepare enough molds before starting.
- Plastic wrap
- Waxed paper
- Cookie cutters are also useful to cut soap into pretty shapes.

Different types of soaps require different ingredients, so it is best to check each recipe beforehand to make sure you know exactly what you will need. The base products and some of the other ingredients need to be purchased from a specialist supplier (see pages 126–127). A list of basic ingredients is below:

- Base oils: coconut, soya bean, light olive oil (not extra virgin)
- Caustic soda (cold-pressed soaps only)
- Soap flakes, liquid soap base, shower gel base, bubble bath base
- Block glycerin
- A range of essential oils
- Herbs, dried flowers, oats, rosehip granules, and spices for natural colors and textures
- Nutrients to enrich the soaps, including shea butter, cocoa butter, almond oil, avocado oil, jojoba oil, rosehip oil, beeswax, Monoi de Tahiti, honey, liquid glycerin.

Basic Techniques

Making cold-process soap is complex, but don't fret. These instructions supplement the individual recipes to give you the best chance of success.

Cold-process soap is based on saponification, meaning a chemical reaction between an acid (oils) and a base (lye). The acid and the base combine to form a syrupy mixture, which is poured into molds to set. Attaining the correct temperature is essential to this process, and the oils and lye must be the same temperature when mixed, between 95°F (35°C) and 100°F (38°C). This is not so simple, because when you add caustic soda to water it heats up to well over 100°F (38°C), so you need to let it cool while you heat the oils.

It is helpful to have a bowl of cold water standing by so you can cool the lye to match the temperature of the oils. Similarly, if the oils heat too much, you can cool them in the same manner.

Add the lye to the oils, pouring slowly and stirring continuously. Be careful to avoid splashing. Once all the lye has been added, keep stirring the mixture until it starts to trace. Tracing occurs when the mixture has become opaque and thick enough to drizzle a pattern on the surface of the soap and not have it sink in. Be careful not to stir too vigorously—which will create air bubbles—but briskly enough to mix the two liquids thoroughly.

Tracing usually occurs between fifteen minutes and a couple of hours, depending on the recipe. Be patient. If tracing hasn't happened after an hour, leave the mixture off the heat and stir it occasionally. If the balance of oils to lye wasn't quite accurate, or if the two were not exactly the same temperature, then tracing may take up to forty-eight hours. If it hasn't happened by then, it won't, so throw the mixture away and start again.

After tracing, you can add essential oils, color, nutrients, and other ingredients to give the soap texture. Make sure ingredients such as dried flowers or oats are finely ground. Also ensure that nutrients such as honey are warmed slightly so the warm, saponified soap mixture isn't "shocked" by adding cold substances.

Once you've added the ingredients and nutrients, prepare the molds by lightly greasing them with oil, making it easy to remove the soap from the molds. Slowly pour the liquid into your molds, cover the molds with plastic wrap or cardboard, place them somewhere warm, and cover with blankets. This ensures the soap cools slowly and allows the saponification process to continue. After twenty-four hours uncover the molds and let them sit for four to seven days.

Check the soap regularly. When it's hard enough to cut and retain its shape, remove it from the mold. If you used a large mold, cut the soap into individual bars. You must still wear rubber gloves, as the saponification is not complete and the caustic could still irritate your skin. Let the soap sit in a warm, dry place for three to four weeks, turning once halfway through. This is the final curing process, during which the soap becomes hard and mild, and is then ready to use.

Tip: *A grooved wooden honey spoon is a particularly useful tool for measuring the honey into the bowl, as it can help avoid dripping honey everywhere.*

2 Essential Oils and Natural Colors

Essential Oils Profiles

Essential oils are nature's gift. They are distilled from the naturally occurring essences in aromatic plants. Many essential oils are distilled from organically grown plants, and these oils are the best to fragrance your soaps. Below is a list of the main essential oils used in the recipes, together with a description of their fragrances. A "P" indicates the oil should not to be used during pregnancy. An "S" indicates possible skin irritation for people with sensitive skin.

Basil/Holy Basil (ocimum basilicum/sanctum)
Basil is a familiar culinary herb. The essential oil has sweet, green, herbaceous top notes and spicy, licorice undertones. Holy basil has a similar aroma, but has a deeper fragrance. *P*

Bergamot (citrus bergamia)
Bergamot is grown in Italy, and is the finest of the citrus oils. It has sweet, lemon, fresh top notes and warm, floral, balsamic undertones. *S*

Chamomile Roman/Chamomile German (anthemis nobilis/matricaria chamomilla)
Chamomile is a well-known herbal tea. The essential oil has hints of apple among bitter, herbaceous undertones and warm, flowery top notes. *P*

Frankincense (boswellia carteri)
Frankincense literally smells divine, and was traditionally burnt as an offering to the gods. It combines citrus and turpentine top notes with undertones of camphor and balsamic wood smoke.

Geranium (pelargonium gravolens)
Geranium smells a little like rose, but is much less expensive to produce, and is used in the perfume industry to "extend" rose. It has light, green top notes and soft, rosy, floral undertones. *P*

Ginger (zingiber officinalis)
Ginger is used in cooking and teas as a stimulating, fortifying digestive. The essential oil has sharp, green top notes and fiery, woody, sweet, spicy undertones. *S*

Jasmine (jasminum officinale)
Jasmine has a powerful, heady fragrance that some people find overwhelming, but once diluted it becomes more subtle. Jasmine has sweet, floral, exotic top notes and heady, warm, honeyed undertones. *P*

Lavender (lavandula vera)
Lavender is the most popular and widely used essential oil, and is reminiscent of traditional English gardens. Lavender

has clean, fresh, floral top notes and subtle, green, herbaceous undertones.

Lemon (citrus limon)

The fresh smell of lemon is widely used in cleaning products, so it is also excellent in soaps. Lemon has clean, fresh, sharp top notes with slightly sweet undertones. **S**

Neroli/Orange Blossom (citrus bigardia/aurantium)

Traditionally used in wedding bouquets, neroli calms and soothes. The delightful fragrance has delicate, fresh, floral top notes and warm, heady, bittersweet undertones.

Orange (citrus sinensis)

This essential oil is distilled from the sweet orange variety. Known as the "smiley oil," orange smells familiar, joyful, and warming. Orange has sweet, fresh, fruity top notes and radiant, sensuous undertones.

Rose (rosa centifolia/damascena)

Romantic rose has been described as the queen of flowers. The different varieties share a similar scent. Rose has sweet, floral top notes with dusky, honeyed undertones. **P**

Rosemary (rosmarinus officinalis)

"Rosemary for remembrance" is an old folk saying, and rosemary is a mental stimulant. Rosemary has sharp, fresh, green, top notes and strong herbaceous, camphoraceous undertones. **P**

Rosewood (aniba rosaeodora)

Rosewood is an endangered species, so make sure any oil you buy comes from a sustainable rosewood plantation. Rosewood is both subtle and powerful with soft, floral top notes and sweet, woody undertones.

Sandalwood (santalum album)

Sandalwood's warm, heavy fragrance increases over time, and it has the longest lasting aroma of essential oils. Sandalwood has sweet, woody, roselike top notes and deep, balsamic, spicy, oriental undertones.

Ylang Ylang (cananga odorata)

Ylang ylang is frequently used in the perfume industry for its voluptuous, exotic fragrance. It has intensely sweet, almond, floral, tropical top notes and slightly cloying, creamy, spicy undertones.

"Common sense and caution should go hand in hand when deciding on the choice of oils and strength of dilution."

—Patricia Davis, *author and aromatherapist*

How to Use Essential Oils Safely

Essential oils are highly concentrated. This is easily demonstrated by the fact that it takes thousands of jasmine petals to produce a single drop of jasmine oil and thousands of rose petals to produce a drop of rose oil. This potency must be respected, and how you handle essential oils is important. Following the guidelines below ensures you can use essential oils safely to perfume your soaps and to create scents.

- Because essential oils are powerful and highly concentrated, they can be toxic if used incorrectly. However, if you handle oils carefully and follow these simple guidelines, they are safe.

- Never take essential oils orally. It is illegal for even a qualified aromatherapist to suggest this. Avoid all contact with the mouth and eyes.

- Some essential oils can cause skin irritation if they are applied undiluted to the skin; therefore this is not recommended. Only apply properly diluted essential oils to the skin.

- The profiles of essential oils (see pages 24–25) lists which oils might cause skin irritation for those with sensitive skin. Occasionally, a slight redness or itchiness might occur from using these or any other essential oil. If this happens, apply some base cream or base oil, such as almond, to the affected area, and place a cold, wet cloth on the affected area until the redness or itchiness disappears.

- Do not increase the amount of essential oils used in the recipes, and make sure you follow the instructions carefully.

- If you accidentally splash a drop of essential oil in your eyes, use a small amount of base oil to dilute the essential oil, and absorb this with a soft cloth before rinsing the eyes with lots of cold water.

- A few essential oils, such as bergamot and the other citrus oils, are phototoxic. This means they might cause skin discoloration in bright sunlight, though once incorporated into soap they are diluted and quite safe. Be careful when applying scents containing bergamot if the weather is hot and sunny, although dabbing the scent behind your ears is fine.

Color Your Soaps

There are many different ways to color soaps, but some are artificial and unpleasant. Bright green, vibrant purple, and deep pink soaps are colored with synthetic chemicals, and come with possible health risks. However, it is surprisingly easy to use natural, organic herbs and spices to color your soaps, and a few essential oils give color, too. You will not obtain the bright, uniform colors achieved with synthetics, but instead you will get warm, earthy, unevenly colored, and natural-looking soaps.

On the right is a list of natural ingredients with which to color your soaps. Because you are working with natural and organic substances, there is no guarantee of exact color, but the variations and new discoveries are part of the fun of making your own soaps. With herbs, spices, and roots, make sure they are finely ground. Then stir ½ or 1 teaspoon full into 2 teaspoons of heated vegetable oil. Mix well, and then filter out larger particles with a tea strainer or coffee filter before mixing into the soap. When using essential oils, remember they will also perfume your soaps. First mix in ten drops and, if you want a stronger shade of color, keep adding drops one by one till you get the desired shade.

Color	Ingredient
Yellow	Turmeric
Orange	Turmeric and Paprika
Red/Mauve	Alkanet Root
Pink	Rosehip Granules
Blue	Blue Chamomile or Blue Cypress essential oil
Green	Blue Chamomile and Turmeric
Brown	Cinnamon
Peach	Paprika

These are a few basic ideas to get you started. Don't be afraid to experiment with other natural ingredients, and by varying the quantities of colorant and oil you will achieve different shades, tones, and colors.

Tip: *Try swirling the color in briefly, rather than mixing it in thoroughly. This will give you an attractive rippled effect rather than a uniformly colored soap.*

3 Liquid Soaps, Bath Bombs, Bubble Baths, and Shower Gels

Getting Started

This chapter contains some really simple recipes to get you started on the soap maker's path. The recipes for liquid soaps, bubble baths, and shower gels require cosmetic base products, which you can easily purchase from the list of specialist suppliers (see pages 126–127). Some stores that offer natural, herbal remedies and essential oils are also beginning to sell a few base products for homemade soaps and cosmetics.

Don't be put off by the long list of strange ingredients in the base products. These are just the proper technical or chemical terms. For example, aqua simply means water.

When purchasing base products, make sure they contain no fragrances and are uncolored. Cosmetic bases should ideally be vegetable oil or water based, so essential oils will mix in easily.

Liquid soaps can be made by simply mixing the base with essential oils and a color base, if desired. You can experiment with your own favorite blends of essential oils and try out different natural colors. Once you feel confident with your experimenting, you can even add a few drops of herbal tinctures to add different healing qualities.

Bath bombs, or bath tablets, make a wonderfully scented and exuberant fizz when they hit water. Easy to make and fun to use, bath bombs bring out the inner child. A key ingredient, baking soda, is more familiar in the kitchen for baking cakes but has traditionally also been used in bathing to calm irritated skin.

Bubble baths and shower gels are made in a similar way to liquid soaps, by simply mixing in essential oils and color. The recipes given here are a good start, but you can also experiment to create your own personalized bathing products.

Make sure you use a large enough container to stir essential oils and colors into the base thoroughly without spilling over. Mix steadily, but not too vigorously; you don't want too many bubbles until the soap or bubble bath is being used.

The best tool for mixing essential oils and colors into the base products is a glass stirring rod. Specially designed for this purpose, you can purchase a glass stirring rod from one of the specialist suppliers listed (see pages 126–127) or a kitchen-supply store. Alternatively, you can use a wooden or plastic chopstick.

"By purchasing fine-quality essential oils and absolutes, along with natural base products, you will be able to create recipes that are natural, fragrant, gentle, and easy to follow."

–Janita Morris, *author and scent maker*

Did You Know? *Citrus essential oils are obtained by a technique called expression, which means simply squeezing the fruit peel to extract the naturally occurring essential oil. This is quite easy to do at home, and you could substitute all or some of the essential oil with some you expressed yourself from fresh, organic citrus fruits.*

Liquid Soaps

Liquid soaps are equally popular in the kitchen and the bathroom. They are most easily used in a pump dispenser bottle. One of the great advantages of liquid soaps in pump dispenser bottles is that they are completely hygienic. Each squirt is fresh and untouched by anyone else, unlike traditional bars of soap, which are handled by every bather. This makes them the best choice for public bathrooms, restaurant kitchens, and other places where hygiene is at a premium.

Liquid soaps are quite a recent innovation, but their popularity and hygienic qualities have ensured that their use is now widespread. The hygienic quality of liquid soaps can be enhanced by the addition of essential oils such as tea tree, a powerful bactericide and antiseptic, although all essential oils are natural antiseptics to some degree. This means that you can make floral and herbal liquid soaps and know that they are effectively antiseptic.

Citrus Suds

The fresh, clean smell of citrus oils is a favorite for cleaning products. Here, the tang of lemon and the warmth of orange combine to make a sweet, fresh scent. This recipe also contains a few drops of sandalwood. This gives the soap a deeper, long-lasting scent. Citrus Suds is colored with orange in the recipe below, but you could substitute yellow if you prefer, or leave it uncolored.

what's in it?
8½ fl oz (250 ml) liquid soap base

12 drops lemon

10 drops orange

4 drops grapefruit

4 drops sandalwood

10 drops orange color (see page 28)

how's it made?

1 Pour the liquid soap into a container that holds at least 16 fl oz (500 ml) and has a good pouring spout.

2 Carefully drop in the essential oils, one by one, followed by the color.

3 Mix thoroughly into the liquid soap base. Be careful not to create too many bubbles.

4 Pour the mixture into a bottle or pump dispenser. The Citrus Suds liquid soap is now ready to use.

Lavender Lather

Lavender has been in popular, continuous use for thousands of years in all its different forms of fresh and dried flowers, essential oil, and lavender water. It is also a prime ingredient of traditional potpourri. One use that may be familiar to many readers is the lavender sachets that are moth repellent and freshening. Our grandmother's generation used to make them each summer and place them in wardrobes and clothes chests. Another traditional use of lavender is to fragrance soap.

what's in it?

8½ fl oz (250 ml) liquid soap base

20 drops lavender

5 drops geranium

5 drops rosemary

how's it made?

1 Pour the liquid soap into a container that holds at least 16 fl oz (500 ml) and has a good pouring spout.

2 Carefully drop in all the essential oils, one by one.

3 Mix thoroughly into the liquid soap base. Be careful not to create too many bubbles.

4 Pour the mixture into a bottle or pump dispenser. The Lavender Lather liquid soap is now ready to use.

Did You Know? *The name of lavender comes from the Latin word lavare, which means "to wash." Lavender is a natural antiseptic and was used to cleanse wounds as well as for personal washing and laundry.*

Did You Know? *Dead Sea salts have a well-known reputation for their therapeutic qualities. They are traditionally used in bath and spa products to deeply cleanse and revitalize the skin.*

Moisturizing Bath Bombs

Bath bombs are one of the new additions to bath time products. Their fizz has a really contemporary feel. Yet they are similar to, and based on, the old-fashioned bath tablets that were fashionable a couple of decades ago. Moisturizing bath bombs are different: They don't fizz when they hit the bath water, but sink and then melt, releasing their fragrance and moisturizing oils.

The purpose of moisturizing bath bombs is to provide a richly perfumed, healing softness to the bath water. You can soak, relax, and luxuriate in the silky scented water, while letting the healing qualities of the essential oils, Dead Sea salts, and baking soda soften your skin, and the Monoi de Tahiti moisturize your whole body. Moisturizing bath bombs are a wonderful bath time treat.

Tropical Tang

These bath bombs make a luxuriating bath time treat, and the addition of rosehip granules gives them a delicate, flecked appearance. The fresh smell of bergamot, with just a hint of basil, first arises as the bath bomb melts into the water. Then the calming fragrance of lavender combines with the sensuous aroma of rose to encourage you to lie back and relax.

what's in it?
4 oz (100 gm) baking soda

4 oz (100 gm) Dead Sea salts, finely ground

1 tsp orris root powder

1 heaping tsp laundry starch

½ tsp rosehip granules

3 tbsp Monoi de Tahiti

10 drops rose

10 drops bergamot

10 drops lavender

3 drops basil

how's it made?

1 Place the baking soda, sea salts, orris root powder, and laundry starch in a bowl. Add the rosehip granules and mix thoroughly.

2 Gently warm the Monoi de Tahiti in a double boiler until melted. Add to the dry ingredients, along with the essential oils, and stir well.

3 Spoon or pour the thick, viscous mixture into small, flexible molds. This recipe makes eight bath bombs. Place the molds in the freezer for half an hour.

4 Remove from the molds and leave in a cool, dark place overnight. The bombs will be ready to use in the morning.

Exotic Fizz

Using a base of Monoi de Tahiti gives these moisturizing bath bombs a delicious, exotic perfume. Monoi de Tahiti is a soft, white, waxy substance that comes in a block and melts easily when gently heated. It has the wonderful aroma of gardenia flowers combined with the skin-moisturizing qualities of coconut oil.

what's in it?

4 oz (100 gm) baking soda

4 oz (100 gm) Dead Sea salts, finely ground

1 tsp orris root powder

1 heaping tsp laundry starch

½ tsp finely ground chamomile flowers

3 tbsp Monoi de Tahiti

10 drops rosewood

8 drops chamomile

8 drops lemon

7 drops lime

how's it made?

1 Place the baking soda, sea salts, orris root powder, and laundry starch in a bowl. Add the chamomile flowers and mix thoroughly.

2 Gently warm the Monoi de Tahiti in a double boiler until melted. Add to the dry ingredients, along with the essential oils, and stir well.

3 Spoon or pour the thick, viscous mixture into small, flexible molds. This recipe makes eight bath bombs. Place the molds in the freezer for half an hour.

4 Remove from the molds and leave in a cool, dark place overnight. The bombs will be ready to use in the morning.

Tip: *If your molds are too large to make these small moisturizing bath bombs, either half fill the molds, or cut the bath bombs into smaller portions once they have hardened.*

Tip: *To make using Scented Salvation a really relaxing experience, place lighted candles around the bath and turn off the lights. You can play soothing music quietly in the background while you lie back in the warm scented water and let the troubles of the day float away.*

Bubble Baths

Bubble baths are the most familiar of all the bath additives. Their scented, foaming bubbles allow you to lie back and let the soapy water gently float the dirt away. You don't have to scrub yourself down, and you can even do away with using a soap bar altogether if you like.

The popularity of bubble baths means there are many different kinds available. However, the majority of these contain synthetic perfumes and bright chemical colors. These may look good, but they have no real healing qualities and can be harsh on the skin.

Making your own bubble bath is quick and easy, and means you can utilize the healing properties of essential oils and bathe in harmony with nature.

Scented Salvation

We all need rescuing from life's tribulations sometimes, and a bath of Scented Salvation will help you relax. After a long, hard day, the soothing aroma of this bubble bath will float away all your stress and irritability. The sweet, heady fragrance of ylang ylang combines with the clear, calming scent of lavender to help prepare you for sleep. Frankincense helps you breath deeply and let go of stress, while the grapefruit and ginger lift your spirits.

what's in it?
8½ fl oz (250 ml) bubble bath base
9 drops lavender
8 drops ylang ylang
8 drops frankincense
6 drops grapefruit
5 drops ginger
2 drops sandalwood
2 drops jasmine

(Don't worry if you don't have all the essential oils mentioned, as any combination of the above oils will make a delightful, relaxing bath.)

how's it made?
1 Pour the bubble bath base into a container that holds at least 16 fl oz (500 ml) and has a good pouring spout.

2 Carefully drop in the essential oils, one by one, making sure you don't lose count of the drops.

3 Mix the oils thoroughly into the bubble bath base. Be careful not to create too many bubbles. You will see the bubble bath base change slightly. It might seem to turn a little thicker as you stir in the oils, and it will change from clear to opaque.

4 Pour the mixture into a pretty glass bottle (you can use a funnel if you'd like) and the Scented Salvation bubble bath is ready to use.

Winter Warmer

This bubble bath is a powerful ally in the fight against colds, influenza, and all the other coughs, cold, and chills of winter. Incorporating essential oils that help fight off infection, Winter Warmer also includes spice essential oils that warm the mind and body. The familiar smell of eucalyptus combines with the potent aroma of peppermint to provide a powerful antidote to a stuffed-up nose. Lavender soothes sore throats and eases the pain of sinusitis and headaches. Bathing with Winter Warmer can help prevent the onset of a cold as well as relieve its symptoms.

what's in it?

8½ fl oz (250 ml) bubble bath base

9 drops lavender

8 drops eucalyptus

6 drops rosemary

6 drops tea tree

3 drops ginger

4 drops peppermint

2 drops black pepper

(Don't worry if you don't have all the essential oils mentioned, as any combination of the above oils will make a warming bath to help fight off colds and the flu.)

how's it made?

1 Pour the bubble bath base into a container that holds at least 16 fl oz (500 ml) and has a good pouring spout.

2 Carefully drop in the essential oils, one by one, making sure you don't lose count of the drops.

3 Mix the oils thoroughly into the bubble bath base. Be careful not to create too many bubbles. You will see the bubble bath base change slightly. It might seem to turn a little thicker as you stir in the oils, and it will change from clear to opaque.

4 Pour the mixture into a pretty glass bottle (you can use a funnel if you'd like) and the Winter Warmer bubble bath is now ready to use.

Did You Know? Tea tree is one of nature's most powerful anti-infectious agents, successfully warding off viruses as well as bacteria and fungi. Tea tree is also an immuno-stimulant. This means it helps the body strengthen its immune system so you are less susceptible to catching viruses.

Did You Know? *Peppermint contains a lot of menthol—an excellent decongestant—so Minty Spice is a good shower gel to use when you have a cold. Peppermint also has a mildly antiseptic effect, which helps deeply cleanse the skin, especially after sweating out the body's toxins.*

Shower Gels

Shower gels are a better alternative to soap bars in the shower. Even while using a draining soap dish, most bars of soap—especially natural, organic vegetable soaps, which tend to be softer than commercially made soaps—will disintegrate quickly and be wasted. Shower gels are equally, if not more, effective than bars of soap and they won't melt away on their own. The addition of essential oils to the shower gel base creates a fresh smelling, pleasant-to-use body wash.

To some extent, shower gel and bubble bath bases are similar, though bubble bath is often made from a thicker base product. The thickness of shower gel and bubble bath depends on which supplier you purchase your base products from. This means shower gel and bubble bath bases can be inter-changed, according to personal preference. It is best to try out both your base products in the bath and the shower, and decide which you like best in each circumstance.

Minty Spice

This recipe is very freshening and deodorant, so it makes a good shower gel to use after lounging in a sauna, playing sports, or partic-ipating in other strenuous activities. The addi-tion of peppermint essential oil gives you a light, tingly feeling all over, while the clean, clear smell of the citrus and spice oils refresh your senses. Minty Spice leaves your skin feeling toned and clean.

what's in it?

8½ fl oz (250 ml) shower gel base

10 drops green color (see page 28)

10 drops palmarosa

10 drops peppermint

8 drops coriander

6 drops lemon

4 drops bergamot

2 drops clove

how's it made?

1 Pour the shower gel base into a container that holds at least 16 fl oz (500 ml) and has a good pouring spout. Add the green color.

2 Carefully drop in all the essential oils, one by one.

3 Mix the oils thoroughly into the shower gel base. Be careful not to create too many bub-bles. The mixture will turn from clear to opaque as you mix in the essential oils.

4 Pour the mixture into a squeeze bottle, or pump-dispenser bottle, and the Minty Spice shower gel is ready to use.

Early Riser

Waking up isn't always that easy, especially after a late night. Early Riser contains essential oils that are fresh smelling and stimulating to wake you up and help you face the day ahead. This shower gel is best used only in the morning, as the stimulating oils are counterproductive for sleep. Even after the heaviest night out, you will feel refreshed and ready to go after a shower with Early Riser.

what's in it?
8½ fl oz (250 ml) shower gel base

10 drops geranium

10 drops bergamot

8 drops rosemary

6 drops petitgrain

4 drops juniper

2 drops basil

how's it made?
1 Pour the shower gel base into a container that holds at least 16 fl oz (500 ml) and has a good pouring spout.

2 Carefully drop in all the essential oils, one by one.

3 Mix the oils thoroughly into the shower gel base. Be careful not to create too many bubbles. The mixture will turn from clear to opaque as you mix in the essential oils.

4 Pour the mixture into a squeeze bottle, or pump-dispenser bottle, and the Early Riser shower gel is ready to use.

Tip: *Plastic squeeze bottles are the traditional containers for shower gels, and they work quite well. However, using a pump-action dispenser bottle is even easier, so that when your hands are slippery with suds you don't have to hold and squeeze the bottle; you need only press the pump dispenser.*

4 Cream Soaps, Hand-Milled Soaps, and Wash Balls

Handcrafted Soaps

In this chapter you will learn how to make a range of simple, handcrafted soaps. The techniques involved in making these soaps are a little more sophisticated than the techniques for making the recipes from the previous chapter, but not quite as demanding as making the cold-process soaps in the next chapter. Cream soaps, hand-milled soaps, and wash balls all provide the opportunity to make your own soaps simply and quickly, yet the finished product can look wonderful and professional if you spend some time and imagination in wrapping and presenting the soaps in creative ways.

Cream soaps are made by using ready-bought soap flakes as the main ingredient. Some soap flakes are derived from professionally produced machine-milled soap that has been grated into fine flakes. Professionally milled soap is made by machines that press freshly made soap between rollers. This process flattens the bar into a very thin sheet, which is then shredded into soap flakes. This flattening and shredding is repeated several times. The mixture is then put through an extruding machine that condenses the mixture into bars of tightly compacted soap so that the individual flakes are no longer discernible.

These bars of soap are what you typically purchase in the drugstore or supermarket. The bars of soap are very hard and have a polished appearance, and the milling process has given the soaps a quick and easy lathering quality. These bars of soap can withstand being dropped in the bath or basin without disintegrating. However, the majority of machine-milled soaps are made from beef tallow and various synthetic additives. This means that they are not of pure vegetable origin nor are they organic—a good reason to ensure that you buy only natural, vegetable-based soap flakes.

Making your own hand-milled soap is both simple and creative. Start by purchasing some bars of unscented, uncolored vegetable soap. Using a kitchen grater, grate the bars to produce fine curls of soap that are easy to melt down. Making hand-milled soap is also a great way to use up any leftover pieces of quality soap that have become too small to use.

The wash balls recipes in this book are derived and adapted from one of the early, more traditional forms of soap. Before commercially produced soap became available, wash balls were traditionally used in both the kitchen and bathroom, for all washing and laundry purposes. The coarsest and most basic wash balls would be used to launder clothes and linens, while the more elaborate soap balls—often perfumed with flowers, flower waters, and herbs—would be used for personal washing.

Tip: To make a romantic present for a loved one you could place the Honey Rose Dream soap in a pretty box on a bed of dried rose petals.

Cream Soaps

Cream soap recipes are created using soap flakes. You can purchase soap flakes from any of the specialty suppliers on pages 126–127, but they are also available from good quality drugstores. You do need to check that the soap flakes you purchase are made purely from soap with no detergent, color, or perfume added.

The soap flakes are slowly melted with liquid glycerin (and sometimes a base oil, such as almond oil) over a double boiler. The addition of a base oil makes a lighter weight soap. Once all the flakes have melted, the mixture is removed from the heat and essential oils, natural colors, and any other ingredients are added. Finally, the mixture is whipped either with a hand whisk or an electric beater. This makes the soap light and creamy, but it thickens in just a few minutes. As soon as the mixture has thickened, spoon the cream soap into a greased mold and leave it to set in a cool place.

Honey Rose Dream

The healing qualities of honey are incorporated in this mild soap, which makes the soap soft and sweet. The addition of rosehip granules gives the soap a delicate pinky-peach color and the voluptuous scent of roses makes it smell like a dream.

what's in it?

8 oz (225 gm) soap flakes
6¾ fl oz (200 ml) rose water
1 tbsp (15 ml) honey
1 tbsp (15 ml) almond oil
1 tbsp (10 ml) liquid glycerin
1 large tsp rosehip granules
25 drops rose
10 drops neroli
10 drops chamomile
5 drops frankincense

how's it made?

1 Place the soap flakes, rosewater, honey, almond oil, and glycerin over a double boiler and heat until the soap flakes melt. Stir with a glass stirring rod or chopstick to blend the mixture thoroughly.

2 Add the rosehip granules and stir. The mixture will turn a pinky-peach color.

3 Remove from the heat and carefully drop in the essential oils, one by one, and then whisk the mixture with an electric beater until it thickens, in a few minutes.

4 Quickly spoon the mixture into a greased mold, and smooth off with the back of a spoon dipped in hot water.

5 Let set for an hour, or until the soap is firm to the touch, and then turn it out of the mold.

6 Leave to dry on waxed paper for two to three weeks. The Honey Rose Dream cream soap will then be ready to use.

Indian Promise

This soap is left uncolored so you end up with a pale, creamy, natural-looking soap. The exotic scent is reminiscent of the Orient, with its warm, spicy fragrance. The addition of jojoba oil makes a light soap with excellent moisturizing qualities, so this is a good soap to use if you have dry skin.

what's in it?

8 oz (225 gm) soap flakes

6¾ fl oz (200 ml) orange flower water

2 tbsp (25 ml) jojoba oil

1 tbsp (10 ml) liquid glycerin

1 tbsp (5 ml) cocoa butter

20 drops sandalwood

10 drops ginger

5 drops coriander

5 drops cinnamon

5 drops lemongrass

5 drops vanilla

how's it made?

1 Place the soap flakes, orange flower water, jojoba oil, and glycerin over a double boiler. Heat gently until the soap flakes start to melt. Stir with a glass stirring rod or chopstick to blend the mixture thoroughly.

2 Melt the cocoa butter in a small saucepan, and add to the melted ingredients.

3 Remove from the heat and carefully drop in the essential oils, one by one, and then whisk the mixture with an electric beater until it thickens, in a few minutes.

4 Quickly spoon the mixture into a greased mold, and smooth off with the back of a spoon dipped in hot water.

5 Let set for an hour, or until the soap is firm to the touch, and then turn it out of the mold.

6 Leave to dry on waxed paper for two to three weeks the Indian Promise cream soap will then be ready to use.

Did You Know? *Traditionally, spices (and thus their scents) are used to stimulate the appetite. Many of the essential oils used in Indian Promise are also used in Indian and other Asian cooking. Sandalwood has been used in India for centuries in Ayurvedic skin care preparations and to perfume soap.*

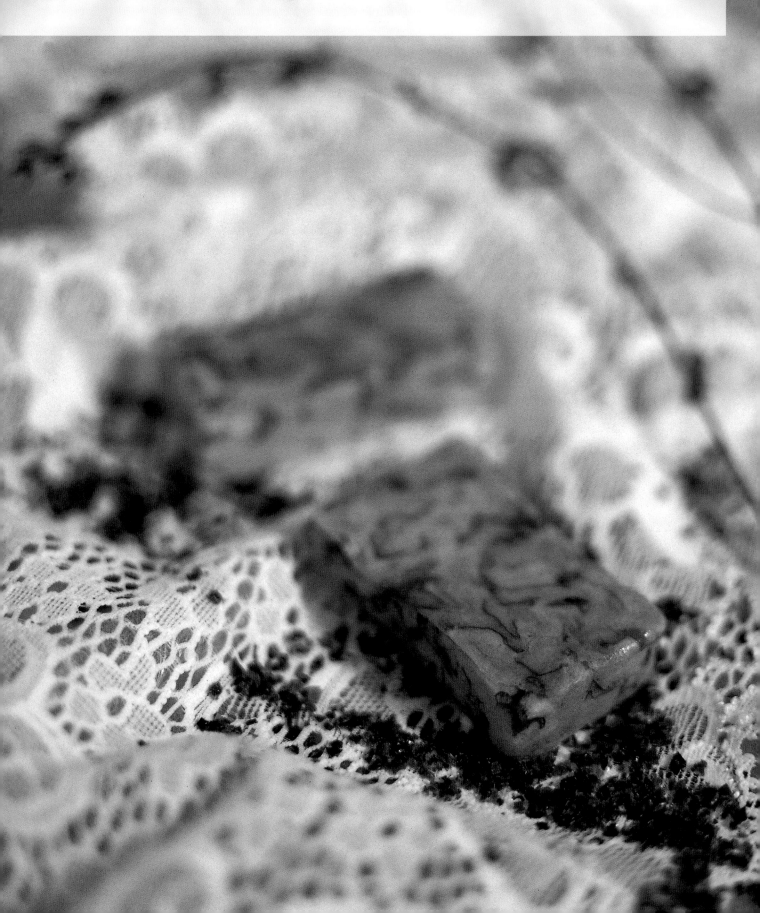

Tip: *The addition of rose petals gives a marbled, textured effect to the Summer Seduction hand-milled soap.*

Hand-Milled Soaps

In addition to grating bars of soap and recycling leftover soap pieces, you can also use the trimmings from your soap making efforts to make hand-milled soap. It doesn't take long to accumulate enough leftovers and trimmings to make a batch of hand-milled soap. However, when you use leftover soap scraps and trimmings, remember to add less essential oils and colors, as these scraps of soap are already colored and perfumed.

Homemade hand-milled soap produces a softer, fluffier, and less durable soap. However, making and using your own natural soap is more pleasurable than using the longer-lasting, synthetic, store-bought variety. These recipes include various additions to make colored, textured, and fragrant soaps. Once you have made a few batches of soap, you can then experiment with different ingredients. In this way, you can create your own personalized hand-milled soaps.

Summer Seduction

This sweet smelling soap has a romantic pinky-peach color because of the addition of rosehip granules. Shea butter is also known as African karite butter. It soothes and softens dry or chapped skin and nourishes all skin types. The inclusion of shea butter makes a gentle soap that is suitable for people with sensitive skin.

what's in it?

18 fl oz (530 ml) water	1 tsp (5 gm) rose petals or dried
1 tbsp (10 gm) rosehip	rosebuds (optional)
granules	20 drops rosewood
8 oz (225 gm) grated,	10 drops rose
unscented, uncolored,	10 drops bergamot
vegetable-based soap	10 drops patchouli
1 oz (30 ml) beeswax	5 drops ylang ylang
1 oz (30 ml) shea butter	5 drops vetiver

how's it made?

1 Grease enough molds for approximatley twelve bars of soap with a little sunflower oil. Put the water in the top half of a double boiler. If you don't have a double boiler, you can fit a small saucepan inside a bigger one. Add the rosehip granules and grated soap slowly, stirring gently as you mix the soap into the water.

2 Either let the soap melt thoroughly, stirring frequently, or alternatively, pour into a blender and blend until the mixture is smooth. You may need to add a little more water.

3 When the soap is fully melted, add the beeswax and shea butter. Stir until melted. If you blended the soap and water, pour back into the pan and stir gently to remove as much air as possible. Then add the beeswax and shea butter.

4 Remove from the heat and gently stir in the rose petals, if using. Finally, add the essential oils and incorporate them into the mixture.

5 Pour the soap into the greased molds, and cover with plastic wrap. After twenty-four hours, remove the plastic wrap and place molds in a warm, dry place for another twenty-four hours. Then take the soap bars out of the molds and place on waxed paper.

6 If you used one large mold, after a week, trim the top, bottom, and edges of the block of soap and cut into individual bars. Check the soap bars are drying out and hardening nicely every ten days or so, and flip them. Trim off any discolored or uneven edges. The soap will be ready in about three weeks.

Oatmeal and Honey

This is a gently exfoliating, soothing soap, and an enduring, traditional favorite. Oatmeal adds texture to the lather and helps you gently scrub away dead skin cells. Honey hydrates, soothes, and moisturizes the skin. Cocoa butter is rich, soothing, and softening.

what's in it?

18 fl oz (530 ml) water

8 oz (225 gm) grated, unscented, uncolored, vegetable-based soap

1 oz (30 ml) beeswax

1 oz (30 ml) cocoa butter

1 tbsp (15 gm) finely ground oatmeal

1 tbsp (15 ml) gently warmed honey

5 drops vanilla

20 drops nutmeg

20 drops sandalwood

15 drops orange

how's it made?

1 Grease enough molds for approximately twelve bars of soap with a little sunflower oil. Put the water in the top half of a double boiler, and heat until nearly boiling. If you don't have a double boiler, you can fit a small saucepan inside a bigger one. Add the grated soap slowly, stirring gently as you mix the soap into the water.

2 Grated soap can take an hour or so to melt thoroughly and requires frequent stirring. Alternatively, you can stir the mixture for five minutes until you have a glutinous mixture and the grated soap curls are beginning to disintegrate. Then pour into a blender and blend until the mixture is smooth. You may need to add a little more water.

3 When the soap is fully melted, add the beeswax and cocoa butter. Stir until melted. If you blended the soap and water, pour back into the pan and stir gently to remove as much air as possible. Then add the beeswax and cocoa butter.

4 Remove from the heat and pour in the oatmeal, stirring to mix it in thoroughly. Finally add the honey and essential oils and incorporate them into the mixture.

5 Pour the soap into the greased molds and cover with plastic wrap. After twenty-four hours, remove the plastic wrap and place molds in a warm, dry place for another twenty-four hours. Then take the soap bars out of the molds and place on waxed paper.

6 If you used one large mold, after a week, trim the top, bottom, and edges of the block of soap and cut into individual bars. Check the soap bars are drying out and hardening nicely every ten days or so, and flip them. Trim off any discolored or uneven edges. The soap will be ready in about three weeks.

Tip: *Add the gently warmed honey just before the essential oils so the soap has cooled slightly. High temperatures destroy the honey's active properties.*

Did You Know? *Halved lemons were traditionally kept near the kitchen sink and used to rub over the hands to dispel the powerful aroma of onions and garlic. This citrus soap makes a good alternative and is pleasant to use in the kitchen.*

Wash Balls

Wash balls are yet another example of how you can make homemade soap in your kitchen. The recipes below are specially designed to make easily molded wash balls, and the ingredients include binding agents such as laundry starch and orris root powder. Orris root is primarily used in the perfume industry as a fixative, which means that orris root literally anchors the scent into an overall fragrance. When it is used to make wash balls, it both acts as a fixative and as a binding agent.

You can also make soap balls from cold-process soap to achieve a different effect. After about a week during cold-process curing, the soap is firm enough to handle yet soft enough to still be malleable. Simply scoop up a handful of soap and roll into a ball (be sure to wear rubber gloves). To make snow balls, make sure the soap is still quite moist. After shaping it into a ball, roll it in finely shaved white soap. To achieve a different effect, roll it in finely ground flower petals or oatmeal.

Orange Lemon Tang

This sharp and sweet smelling soap contains a combination of citrus essential oils and other lemon- and orange-scented oils. This makes a clean, refreshing perfumed soap with just a hint of floral sweetness.

what's in it?

8 oz (225 gm) soap flakes
1 tsp (5 ml) orris root powder
1 tsp (5 ml) laundry starch
15 drops orange
15 drops lemon
10 drops mandarin
10 drops petitgrain
5 drops lemongrass
5 drops bergamot
5 drops rosewood
5 drops geranium
1 tbsp (15 ml) almond oil
1 tbsp (10 ml) orange or yellow color, according to preference (see page 28)
5 tbsp (75 ml) hot orange flower water

how's it made?

1 Grind the soap flakes with a pestle and mortar until you have a fine, gritty powder. Pour into a mixing bowl.

2 Add the orris root powder and laundry starch and mix well. Add the essential oils to the almond oil, then add to the dry ingredients, along with the color of your choice, and mix well.

3 Add the hot orange flower water to the bowl and mix everything together well with a fork.

4 As the mixture starts to bind, use your hands to knead it until you achieve a uniform, pliable dough. Divide the mixture into three roughly equal-sized pieces and roll into balls.

5 Grease your hands lightly with sunflower oil and continue to mold the balls until all irregularities are smoothed out.

6 Place on waxed paper in a warm, dry space for five days. The Orange Lemon Tang wash balls will then be ready to use.

Chocolate Spice

Using real, organic chocolate makes these wash balls smell delicious, and almost good enough to eat. The chocolate and the ground cinnamon give the soap a lovely, rich, earthy brown color. If you have children around, make sure they know these Chocolate Spice wash balls are soap and are not edible!

what's in them?

8 oz (225 gm) soap flakes

1 tbsp (15 ml) organic cocoa or dark chocolate powder

1 tsp (5 ml) laundry starch

2 tbsp (25 ml) apricot kernel oil

½ tsp (2.5 ml) ground cinnamon

10 drops nutmeg

10 drops cinnamon

5 drops cardamon

5 drops vanilla

5 tbsp (75 ml) hot water

how're they made?

1 Grind the soap flakes with a pestle and mortar until you have a fine, gritty powder. Pour into a mixing bowl.

2 Add the cocoa powder and laundry starch and mix well. Add the essential oils to the apricot kernel oil, add to the dry ingredients, and mix well.

3 Add the hot water to the bowl and mix everything together well with a fork.

4 As the mixture starts to bind, use your hands to knead it until you achieve a uniform, pliable dough. Divide the mixture into three roughly equal-sized pieces and roll into balls.

5 Grease your hands lightly with sunflower oil and continue to mold the balls until all irregularities are smoothed out.

6 Place on waxed paper in a warm, dry space for five days. The Chocolate Spice wash balls will then be ready to use.

Tip: *Washing or bathing with milk was a traditional way of keeping the skin soft. Most famously, Cleopatra bathed in asses' milk. To make a creamy milk chocolate soap, substitute goat's milk, cow's milk, or oat milk for the water.*

Tip: *When you mix in the red color with your fingers, be prepared for pinky-red stains on your fingertips from the strong color base. This will fade in a day or two, or can be scrubbed off with a soapy nail brush.*

Purple Marble

These dramatic looking wash balls have lovely alternating swirls of purple and peachy pink. The marbled effect is created by mixing in the color at the end, after the soap is made. The scent is rich and deep, with resinous and woody undertones, together with light, fresh, and sweet floral top notes.

what's in it?

8 oz (225 gm) soap flakes

1 tsp (5 ml) orris root powder

1 tsp (5 ml) laundry starch

1 tbsp (10 ml) shea butter, melted

15 drops frankincense

15 drops sandalwood

10 drops patchouli

10 drops geranium

10 drops bergamot

5 drops rose

5 drops ylang ylang

5 tbsp (75 ml) hot rose water

2 tbsp (25 ml) red color (see page 28)

how's it made?

1 Grind the soap flakes with a pestle and mortar until you have a fine, gritty powder. Pour into a mixing bowl.

2 Add the orris root powder and laundry starch and mix well. Add the essential oils to the dry ingredients, along with the hot melted shea butter, and mix well.

3 Pour the hot rose water into the bowl and mix everything together well with a fork.

4 As the mixture starts to bind, use your hands to knead it until you achieve a uniform, pliable dough. Add the red color and blend into the dough with your fingertips to create a marbled effect. Divide the mixture into three roughly equal-sized pieces and roll into balls.

5 Grease your hands lightly with sunflower oil and continue to mold the balls until all irregularities are smoothed out.

6 Place on waxed paper in a warm, dry space for five days. The Purple Marble wash balls will then be ready to use.

5 Glycerin Soaps and Cold-Process Vegetable Soaps

Making Real Soap

The cold-process vegetable soaps in this chapter are the most complicated to make. They take time and effort, and you might need to practice a few batches to get the hang of the process. Nonetheless, making your own natural soap from scratch is a really rewarding activity. Once you have made and used a successful batch of hand-crafted soap, you may find you never again want to buy commercially produced soap.

As the quotation on page 70 suggests, it is helpful for the newcomer to soap making to learn as much as possible at first. One of the most important ideas to keep in mind is how to choose your basic ingredients. This book advocates the organic, natural philosophy, and uses organic and vegetable-based ingredients. Ingredients for commercially made soap are usually selected for cheapness and the physical properties they will bring to the finished soap. However, you can choose organic base ingredients that first and foremost have good skin-care properties. It is a good idea to read about the different skin-care qualities of the wide range of base oils and nutrients now available.

The quotation also encourages you to be creative once you've learned the basic techniques of making soap. Soap making can be an art form if you invest the process with the vision, creative impulse, and passion of the artist. Beautiful soaps, presented in unusual and attractive packaging, can adorn a bathroom—alongside being useful, of course!

They also make wonderful gifts, and there are ideas on how to display, wrap, and present your soaps in chapter seven (see pages 108–117).

Don't worry if some batches of cold-process soap don't work out. The most important thing is to figure out and understand why something went wrong. In this way, you can try not to repeat the mistake again. However, making soap involves a little magic and luck, and even the most experienced soap maker can end up with a batch of soap that's not quite right, or even a complete flop. There is a section on troubleshooting at the end of the book that explains why common problems happen and how to avoid them (see page 122).

Making the glycerin soaps is much simpler and quicker, and provides a good contrast to the time and effort involved in making cold-process soap. You could probably start a batch of cold-process soap and during the time it takes to cure and finish, you could have made and used up a bar of glycerin soap! Yet these two different kinds of soap do have something in common that distinguishes them from the previous recipes. Both cold-process and glycerin soaps are made and sold commercially, while all the other soaps are handcrafted specialties that you would be unlikely to find for sale in your local drugstore. So, if soap making really inspires you, perhaps one day you may swell the numbers of cottage industry soap makers.

Glycerin Soaps

Glycerin soaps are increasingly fashionable these days. The first soap ever to be widely advertised was Pears Soap, which is a glycerin soap with a floral and herbal fragrance. Pears fell from favor with the introduction of commercially produced, machine-milled soap. A huge range of these soaps was created and dominated the market. However, with the renewed interest in glycerin soaps, Pears Soap is now proving popular once again.

The process of making glycerin soap is simple: melt a block glycerin, add color and perfume, and allow it to set for an hour or two. This means making these soaps is almost instantly gratifying, and is definitely fun, rather than hard, work. As most of these soaps are nearly transparent, you can add little treasures that are slowly exposed through washing. Little plastic animals, marbles, crystals, and other small ornaments all make decorative and fun additions.

Sweet Hearts

Intriguing and beautiful, these soaps are created by using a flexible, heart-shaped mold, though you can use different shaped molds for other looks if you prefer. These striking soaps are infused with the delicate scent of roses, and the soft, fresh aroma of bergamot. The intense, opaque shade of purple comes from using a lot of red base color.

what's in it?

8 oz (225 gm) grated block glycerin
20 drops red color (see page 28)
20 drops rose
15 drops neroli
15 drops bergamot

how's it made?

1 Grease a heart-shaped mold with a little sunflower oil. Put the grated block glycerin in the top half of a double boiler, or use two saucepans as described on page 59, and heat until melted, stirring gently with a chopstick or glass stirring rod.

2 Remove from the heat and gently stir in the red color, followed by the essential oils. The mixture will turn an intense purple color.

3 Pour the soap into the greased mold. Leave to set for about one and a half hours, or until firm to the touch.

4 Once the soap is set, turn out of the mold. The Sweet Hearts glycerin soap is now ready to use.

Tip: *For extra effect, you can press a single dried rosebud into the surface of the soap just after pouring it into the mold.*

Did You Know? *Many of the herbal essential oils and lavender were used as traditional strewing herbs in the Middle Ages. They were mixed in with rushes and used as floor coverings to keep bad smells and insects away.*

Herbal Garden

The fresh, green aroma of this soap is evocative of a traditional herb garden on a hot summer's day. The addition of blue chamomile gives the soap a delicate, natural blue-green color, as do some types of vetivert. Lavender adds a delicate floral note.

what's in it?

8 oz (225 gm) grated block glycerin

10 drops lavender

5 drops rosemary

5 drops basil

5 drops sweet marjoram

15 drops blue chamomile

10 drops vetivert

how's it made?

1 Grease a mold with a little sunflower oil. Put the grated block glycerin in the top half of a double boiler, or use two saucepans as described on page 59, and heat until melted, stirring gently with a chopstick or glass stirring rod.

2 Remove from the heat and gently stir in the essential oils. The mixture will turn a delicate blue-green color.

3 Pour the soap into the greased mold. Leave to set for about one and a half hours, or until firm to the touch.

4 Once the soap is set, turn out of the mold and trim into whatever shape you like. The Herbal Garden glycerin soap is now ready to use.

Sweet and Spicy

This lovely, fragrant soap will appeal to both women and men. Sweet and Spicy is a good soap to use in the morning, as it has an invigorating, uplifting aroma. The ground cinnamon gives the soap a speckled brown appearance, while the addition of spice essential oils means the soap has a slightly warming effect on the skin.

what's in it?

8 oz (225 gm) grated block glycerin

10 drops ginger

5 drops cardamon

5 drops clove

10 drops cinnamon

10 drops grapefruit

5 drops ylang ylang

5 drops geranium

1 tsp (5 ml) finely ground cinnamon

how's it made?

1 Grease a mold with a little sunflower oil. Put the grated block glycerin in the top half of a double boiler, or use two saucepans as described on page 59, and heat until melted, stirring gently with a chopstick or glass stirring rod.

2 Remove from the heat and gently stir in the essential oils and the ground cinnamon. The mixture will turn a warm, brown color.

3 Pour the soap into the greased mold. Leave to set for about one and a half hours, or until firm to the touch.

4 Once the soap is set, turn out of the mold and trim into whatever shape you like. The Sweet and Spicy glycerin soap is now ready to use.

Marmalade Star

Using a star-shaped cookie cutter makes this a really fun soap to make and wash with. Children especially love using Marmalade Star and they also like helping to make it. The vibrant orange color and the sweet, warm scent of orange combined with slivers of orange peel make this soap reminiscent of marmalade.

what's in it?

8 oz (225 gm) grated block glycerin

50 drops orange

5 drops orange color (see page 28)

1 tsp (5 ml) finely sliced orange peel without the pith

how's it made?

1 Grease a rectangular mold with a little sunflower oil. Put the grated block glycerin in the top half of a double boiler, or use two saucepans as described on page 59, and heat until melted, stirring gently with a chopstick or glass stirring rod.

2 Remove from the heat and gently stir in the essential oil, the orange color, and the slivers of orange peel. The mixture will turn a bright orange color.

3 Pour the soap into the greased mold. Leave to set for about one and a half hours, or until firm to the touch.

4 Once the soap is set, turn out of the mold. Using a star shaped cookie cutter, press firmly down on the soap to cut out two Marmalade Star glycerin soaps. The Marmalade Star is now ready to use.

Tip: *If you prefer the clean, sharp fragrance of lemon to orange, you can make Lemon Star soaps by substituting lemon essential oil for orange, omitting the orange peel, and substituting yellow color for orange.*

Tip: *Soap molds are often beautifully handcrafted from natural substances such as pine wood. They are very sturdy and will last for many batches of soap making.*

Cold-Process Vegetable Soap

Cold-process soap is what most people generally consider as "real" soap. All the other soaps you have read about earlier—and hopefully tried out!—have all included a ready-made soap base of some kind. Whether the base was liquid soap, bubble bath, grated block glycerin, or soap flakes, you still have not yet tried your hand at making soap from scratch. Now the moment has finally arrived.

One reason to try out the other soap recipes first is to develop skill and experience in working with soap. Making soap from scratch does not seem so daunting after making other kinds of soap. You will now be working with the building blocks of soap, the caustic soda (known as lye when it is dissolved in water) and base oils. The fusion of these into soap is a chemical process and is the real magic of making cold-process vegetable soap.

Basic Vegetable Soap

This is a simple soap without any additions, so you can practice this recipe a few times until you feel confident enough to add perfume, nutrients, and color. Be prepared for the odd failure; very few soap makers get it perfect on their first attempt. If your first batch or two don't work and you have to throw them away, at least you have not wasted essential oils and nutrients, which can be expensive. This basic vegetable soap is also lovely to use, and is especially suitable for people with sensitive skin, as there is no fragrance or color.

what's in it?

16 oz (455 gm) distilled water

6 oz (170 gm) of caustic soda

12 oz (340 gm) coconut oil

12 oz (340 gm) light olive oil (not extra virgin)

20 oz (567 gm) soya bean oil

how's it made?

1 Place the water in a lye- and heat-resistant container with a good pouring spout. Wearing rubber gloves and safety glasses or goggles, slowly pour the caustic soda into the water.

2 Gently stir the mixture until all the soda has dissolved, being careful to avoid splashing. The temperature of the lye will soar to well over 100°F (38°C), so leave to one side to cool.

3 Place the coconut oil, olive oil, and soya bean oil in a lye-resistant saucepan and heat gently, stirring to mix thoroughly and to evenly distribute heat. When the temperature is approximately 99°F (37°C), remove from the heat.

4 Keep measuring the temperature of both solutions, and adjust if necessary by using a water bath (see page 20). When both solutions are exactly the same temperature, ideally 97°F (36°C) (although anything between 95°F [35°C] and 100°F [38°C] should work), slowly pour the lye into the oils. You should pour slowly but steadily, stirring gently and often.

5 Once all the lye is combined with the oils, continue to stir constantly but slowly; avoid creating air bubbles. Be sure to mix thoroughly enough to incorporate the two solutions.

6 Be vigilant for signs of tracing—when the mixture turns opaque and thickens. As soon as this happens, pour the soap into greased molds. Seal the mold with plastic wrap, cover with blankets, and place in a warm, dry spot for forty-eight hours.

7 After forty-eight hours, remove the plastic wrap. You now must assess the soap. Remember to wear rubber gloves, as the soap is not yet cured and is still caustic.

8 Gently touch the surface of the soap. If it is still quite soft, leave it to sit unwrapped for another forty-eight hours. If the soap is firm to the touch, but still soft enough to leave an imprint, then unmold the soap carefully.

9 If you used one large mold, trim off any rough or uneven edges, and place on waxed paper to cure. When the soap is quite firm to the touch and pressing on it no longer leaves any imprints, it's time to cut it into individual bars. Start checking after a week.

10 If you used individual molds, once the bars are removed from the molds, place on wax paper to finish curing.

11 In both cases, you need to leave the bars of soap to finish curing in a dry, draft-free place for two to three weeks. After the final curing period, the soap should be hard, just like a commercially bought bar of soap.

12 Scrape off any surface ash that may have come out and trim the bars of soap to make them neat. The soap is now ready to use.

Tip: *Make sure you have plenty of time before you start, as this recipe takes more time than you might expect. Remember that all ingredients, even liquids, are measured as weight and not volume as this is the most accurate. Refer back to Basic Techniques on page 20.*

Tip: *This recipe includes essential oils, but if you prefer unscented soap, this recipe is still luxurious without any added essential oils. Simply leave out the essential oils and carry on with the next step.*

Luxury Soap

This soap contains all the best base oils and most effective nutrients used in soap making. These ingredients make Luxury Soap the best soap possible. It is kind to the skin, protecting and nourishing it, and is a real treat to use. However, the ingredients are expensive, so you probably won't want to make this soap very often. Nonetheless, you—and your friends and family if you are feeling generous!—will appreciate using these gourmet soaps.

what's in it?

16 oz (455 gm) water	8 oz (227 gm) palm oil
6 oz (170 gm) caustic soda	1½ oz (43 gm) shea butter
10½ oz (298 gm) light olive oil	15 drops sandalwood
2 oz (57 gm) apricot kernel oil	15 drops jasmine
2½ oz (71 gm) sweet almond oil	10 drops neroli
2 oz (57 gm) jojoba oil	10 drops orange
2 oz (57 gm) avocado oil	5 drops patchouli
2 oz (57 gm) kukui nut oil	5 drops chamomile
13 oz (369 gm) coconut oil	

how's it made?

1 Place the water in a lye- and heat-resistant container with a good pouring spout. Wearing rubber gloves and safety glasses or goggles, slowly pour the caustic soda into the water.

2 Gently stir the mixture until all the soda has dissolved, being careful to avoid splashing. The temperature of the lye will soar to well over 100°F (38°C), so put it to one side to cool.

3 Place all the base oils, together with the shea butter, in a lye-resistant saucepan and heat gently, stirring to mix thoroughly and to evenly distribute heat. When the temperature is approximately 82°F (28°C), remove from the heat.

4 Keep measuring the temperature of both solutions, and adjust if necessary by using a water bath (see page 20). When both solutions are exactly the same temperature, ideally 80°F (27°C), slowly pour the lye into the oils. You should pour slowly but steadily, stirring gently and often.

5 Once all the lye is combined with the oils, continue to stir constantly but slowly; avoid creating air bubbles. Be sure to mix thoroughly enough to incorporate the two solutions.

6 Be vigilant for signs of tracing—when the mixture turns opaque and thickens. As soon as this happens, drop in the essential oils and stir in thoroughly, then pour the soap into greased molds. Seal the mold with plastic wrap, cover with blankets, and place in a warm, dry spot for forty-eight hours.

7 After forty-eight hours, remove the plastic wrap. You now must assess the soap. Remember to wear rubber gloves, as the soap is not yet cured and is still caustic.

8 Gently touch the surface of the soap. If it is still quite soft, leave it to sit unwrapped for another forty-eight hours. If the soap is firm to the touch, but still soft enough to leave an imprint, then unmold the soap carefully.

9 If you used one large mold, trim off any rough or uneven edges, and place on waxed paper to cure. When the soap is quite firm to the touch and pressing no longer leaves any imprint, it's time to cut it into individual bars. Start checking after a week.

10 If you used individual molds, once the bars are removed from the molds, place on wax paper to finish curing.

11 In both cases, you need to leave the bars of soap to finish curing in a dry, draft-free place for two to three weeks. After this final curing period, the soap should now be hard, just like a commercially bought bar of soap.

12 Scrape off any surface ash that may have come out, and trim the bars of soap to make them neat. The soap is now ready to use.

Rosemary, Geranium, and Lemon

This fresh herbal and citrus smelling soap is a favorite among both sexes. Invigorating rosemary is balanced with geranium, and the addition of lemon gives a refreshing note to the blend. Cocoa butter is a rich emollient that both softens and protects the skin, making this soap a pampering indulgence.

what's in it?

16 oz (455 gm) distilled water	20 drops geranium
6 oz (170 gm) caustic soda	15 drops rosemary
12 oz (340gm) coconut oil	15 drops lemon
12 oz (340 gm) light olive oil	5 drops lavender
(not extra virgin)	5 drops basil
20 oz (565 gm) soya bean oil	5 drops frankincense
1 oz (30 gm) cocoa butter	

how's it made?

1 Follow the instructions for Basic Vegetable Soap (see page 80), adding the cocoa butter in at step 3, until just before tracing begins. Make sure you have the other ingredients close at hand.

2 As soon as the soap starts tracing, add the essential oils. Stir in thoroughly.

3 A variation on this soap is to add a few dried rose or geranium petals, which should be added at this point. This gives the soap a dappled appearance.

4 Follow the instructions for pouring into the mold and curing as you would for the Basic Vegetable Soap.

Cinnamon, Almond, and Honey

This earthy brown soap is laden with organic ground cinnamon, which also makes this soap gently exfoliating. The honey and almond oil add richness to the soap, and both are hydrating and moisturizing for the skin. The spice oils are reminiscent of soft winds over tropical islands. Their fragrance is balanced with a hint of sweetness from the honey and the voluptuous ylang ylang.

what's in it?

16 oz (455 gm) distilled water	2 tsp (10 ml) organic ground
6 oz (170 gm) caustic soda	cinnamon
12 oz (340 gm) coconut oil	15 drops cinnamon
12 oz (340 gm) light olive oil	10 drops clove
(not extra virgin)	10 drops black pepper
20 oz (565 gm) soya bean oil	10 drops grapefruit
1 oz (30 gm) sweet almond oil	10 drops ylang ylang
1 oz (30 gm) warmed honey	5 drops frankincense

how's it made?

1 Follow the instructions for Basic Vegetable Soap (see page 80), until just before tracing begins. Make sure you have the other ingredients close at hand.

2 As soon as the soap starts tracing, add the almond oil, warmed honey, cinnamon, and essential oils. Stir in thoroughly.

3 Alternatively, leave the cinnamon until you have thoroughly mixed in the other ingredients, and simply swirl in at the end to create a marbled effect.

4 Follow the instructions for pouring into the mold and curing as you would for the Basic Vegetable Soap.

Tip: *You can use less cinnamon for a more subtle effect. Adding it at the end and briefly swirling it in gives a marbled mosaic finish, which is very attractive. Experiment with both quantity of cinnamon and technique of adding it to the soap.*

6 Natural Scents

The Art of Perfuming

The art of perfuming has been with us for many centuries, and the ancient civilizations were surprisingly adept at creating scents. There are perfume jars and bottles dating as far back as 3500 BC. Traditionally, perfumes were used for other purposes in addition to personal scents. The most important use of perfume was to please the gods, and perfume in the form of incense was burnt daily so the aromatic smoke would ascend to the heavens.

Aromatic woods, gums, and resins such as frankincense and myrrh were used in the embalming of bodies in ancient Egypt. The ancient Indian medicinal system, Ayurveda, used, and still uses today, sandalwood and saffron in medicinal remedies. Herbs and spices are used throughout the world to scent food and make it appetizing. The overwhelming focus of the perfume industry however is in the arena of personal scents.

The center of the fragrance industry is in Grasse, France. Huge fields of lavender and other flowers and herbs are grown to provide the raw materials for distilling essential oils, one of the prime ingredients of perfumes. Factories for distillation and the creation of perfume are scattered throughout the area. Famous perfume recipes are highly guarded secrets, and each perfume house employs a top "nose"—a highly trained individual who can distinguish between the thousands of different fragrances.

Commercial perfumes are highly complex blends of essential oils, animal derivatives such as musk and ambergris, and high-proof alcohol. It takes a long time to create a fragrance, and hundreds of different ingredients in differing proportions will be tried before one definitive recipe is decided upon. Perfumes are classified into "families," each with a specific character. The most familiar of these are: floral, green, chypre, citrus, aldehydic, oriental, and oceanic. For example, the popular sophisticated modern perfume Opium belongs in the oriental family.

Making your own scents need not be a daunting prospect if you follow a few simple guidelines. All the perfumes in this book use only essential oils, preferably organic, and no animal products. Some perfumes are oil based, and others use alcohol diluted with flower waters. Both these types of perfume are easy to blend. Each perfume needs to have a top note, a middle note, and a base note, to create harmony, like in music. This makes a balanced fragrance that has both an immediate impact and a lasting quality.

Perfuming is an art, and wearing perfume is a personal choice. So after following a few of the following recipes, you could create your own personalized scents. These will reflect your personal creativity, character, and mood. It is intensely satisfying to make and wear your own personal fragrances and it is a creative form of self expression.

"Making scents at home is experimenting with and creating customized fragrances—sprays, essences, perfume oils, colognes, and waters—that blend with and reflect personal emotions, moods, and lifestyles."
                                                —Catherine Bardey, *fashion stylist and author*

Tip: *Oil-based perfumes don't last as long as the alcohol-based perfumes. The rollette bottles are ½ fl oz (10 ml) size and can easily be used up in less than six months. After this time, the perfume will be past its best and may start to degenerate.*

Perfume Roll-ons

Perfume roll-ons are oil-based perfumes dispensed from small roll-on bottles. These are glass bottles with a rollette plastic ball insert; they are easily purchased from one of the suppliers listed on pages 126–127. Perfume roll-ons are both simple to make and convenient to carry in a handbag, so you can freshen up your perfume throughout the day and evening. The four perfume recipes in this section comprise two floral fragrances, one citrus, and one oriental.

Floral is the largest of the perfume families. Floral perfumes suit feminine, delicate personalities, and are especially suited for wearing in the daytime and in the spring and summer. Citrus perfumes are breezy, light, and fresh. They suit the youthful and are exuberantly feminine. They are suited to daytime and casual evening wear. Oriental fragrances are heavy, mysterious, and seductive. They suit the mature, sophisticated personality and are best worn in the evening.

Provence Floral

This delightfully feminine fragrance is influenced by the classic floral perfumes such as L'Air du Temps, Joy, and Chanel No. 22. The light floral essential oils, blended subtly with a little citrus, gives a top note that is light, fresh, and floral. The middle note is deeper, with the calm aroma of chamomile bringing a slightly bitter green note. Hints of frankincense and sandalwood provide a long lasting bottom note, which stabilizes the overall fragrance.

what's in it?

1 tbsp (10 ml) sweet almond oil

10 drops rose

10 drops lavender

10 drops neroli

4 drops mimosa

3 drops geranium

4 drops chamomile

3 drops bergamot

3 drops frankincense

3 drops sandalwood

how's it made?

1 Fill a small glass jar with a lid with 1 tablespoon (10 ml) of sweet almond oil.

2 Line up the bottles of essential oils. If you don't have every one of the essential oils mentioned in the recipe, don't worry. Add the number of drops of the missing oil to one of the other oils, or simply leave them out.

3 Carefully drop in the essential oils, one by one. Shake the jar vigorously, and leave for fifteen minutes for the oils to adjust themselves in the blend.

4 Pour the perfume into a ½ fl oz (10 ml) glass rollette bottle, using a funnel if necessary. Push the roll-on ball in firmly, and screw on the cap. The perfume is now ready to use, but will improve subtly over the next few days.

Fresh and Fruity

This lively, breezy fragrance is ideal for the younger woman, and makes a good first perfume. Neither too heavy nor serious, the delicate fragrance is clean, refreshing, and clear. The citrus oils are complemented by light floral and woody tones. The merest hint of an herbal tone gives a slight green middle note, which balances the citrus top notes.

what's in it?

1 tbsp (10 ml) sweet almond oil

7 drops orange

7 drops mandarin

10 drops bergamot

7 drops petitgrain

5 drops neroli

5 drops rosewood

3 drops clary sage

2 drops ambrette seed

4 drops ylang ylang

Romantic Rose

Roses and rose perfumes have always been among the most popular of fragrances since ancient times. There are quite a few different types of roses grown to produce rose oil, and they all differ slightly. The color of the essential oil ranges from greenish orange to brownish red, and each rose oil will have a slightly different aroma, although it will be unmistakably rose. This perfume uses a few different types of rose oil to give an intense rose fragrance. Rose oil is expensive, so this perfume is a luxurious treat, but if you love roses, this is a wonderful perfume.

what's in it?

1 tbsp (10 ml) sweet almond oil

15 drops rose otto

15 drops rose absolute

10 drops rose geranium

3 drops bergamot

4 drops patchouli

3 drops palmarosa

how're they made?

1 Fill a small glass jar with a lid with 1 tablespoon (10 ml) of sweet almond oil.

2 Line up the bottles of essential oils. If you don't have every one of the essential oils mentioned in the recipes, don't worry. For Romantic Rose, however, you do need to have at least one of the rose oils, but you can adjust the number of drops of each oil according to what you have.

3 Carefully drop in the essential oils, one by one. Shake the jar vigorously, and leave for fifteen minutes for the oils to adjust in the blend.

4 Pour the perfume into a ½ fl oz (10 ml) glass rollette bottle, using a funnel if necessary. Push the roll-on ball in firmly, and screw on the cap. The perfume is now ready to use, but will improve subtly over the next few days.

Did You Know? *Rose oil is probably the most valued essential oil in the perfume industry. Approximately three-quarters of all top-class, quality perfumes on the market today include a percentage of rose oil.*

Did You Know? *The distillation process from which essential oils are derived was probably discovered accidentally by Avicenna, the great Arab physician, during an alchemical experiment with roses.*

Amorous Dreams

This is a mysterious perfume ideal for a roman-
tic evening or a late night party. Deep, sweet,
floral top notes mingle with woody, spicy mid-
dle notes and long lasting earthy, resinous
undertones. Patchouli became popular in the
1960s, and was often worn as a perfume on its
own. Here, it is a lot more subtle, and blended
with floral, citrus, spice, and woody oils to cre-
ate a delightful mystical fragrance.

what's in it?

1 tbsp (10 ml) sweet almond oil

7 drops patchouli

7 drops jasmine

10 drops bergamot

7 drops rose

3 drops vanilla

2 drops myrrh

5 drops sandalwood

3 drops clove

2 drops violet leaf

4 drops nutmeg

how's it made?

1 Fill a small glass jar with a lid with 1 tablespoon (10 ml) of sweet almond oil.

2 Line up the bottles of essential oils. If you don't have every one of the essential oils mentioned in the recipe, don't worry. Add the number of drops of the missing oil to one of the other oils, or sim-ply leave them out.

3 Carefully drop in the essential oils, one by one. Shake the jar vigorously, and leave for fifteen minutes for the oils to adjust themselves in the blend.

4 Pour the perfume into a ½ fl oz (10 ml) glass rol-lette bottle, using a funnel if necessary. Push the roll-on ball in firmly, and screw on the cap. The perfume is now ready to use, but will improve sub-tly over the next few days.

Splash Colognes

Colognes are light, fresh fragrances that are all derived from the traditional eau de cologne. The original eau de cologne was made in the early part of the eighteenth century by Johann-Maria Farina, an Italian living in Cologne, Germany. His cologne quickly became famous for its cooling, deodorant, and refreshing qualities, and by the end of the eighteenth century there were many different versions available.

Commercially made colognes use perfume-grade ethyl alcohol as the base, but this is impossible to purchase in small quantities. For the recipes below, use the highest proof vodka you can find. This is diluted slightly with a flower water, which adds to the overall fragrance, and has a less drying effect on the skin than neat alcohol. As they are not highly concentrated perfumes, you can splash these colognes on generously.

Citrus Cologne

This recipe is a simple version of the original eau de cologne, and has a familiar classic fragrance. The perfume is clean and fresh, with citrus top notes, a light floral middle note, and a green herbal base note.

what's in it?
4 tbsp (50 ml) high proof vodka
40 drops bergamot
25 drops lemon
10 drops neroli
15 drops lavender
10 drops petitgrain
7 drops rosemary
3 drops thyme
2 tbsp (25 ml) orange flower water

how's it made?

1 Fill a dark glass bottle (which can hold 4 fl oz [100 ml] of liquid) with the high proof vodka.

2 Carefully drop in the essential oils, one by one. Put on the bottle cap and shake vigorously for a few minutes to thoroughly dissolve the essential oils.

3 Top off with the flower water, and shake again. A small amount of essential oil may separate out and float on the top, so before using the cologne, remember to shake the bottle first each time.

4 Let the cologne stand for a week or two before using it. This allows the cologne to mature and the perfume to settle.

Did You Know? *Napoleon was notoriously fastidious about personal hygiene, and used lots of eau de cologne. He even took it along and used it during his military campaigns.*

Did You Know? *Colognes were traditionally used to scent handkerchiefs and personal linens as well as being used as personal perfumes.*

Deep and Mysterious

The traditional eau de cologne is suitable for both women and men. Deep and Mysterious has a green, woody, spicy fragrance that might be described as masculine, and is particularly suited to men, though not exclusively of course! Perfume is a personal choice, and you should wear what perfumes you like, whether they are described as suitable for you or not.

what's in it?
4 tbsp (50 ml) high proof vodka
20 drops vetiver
10 drops frankincense
15 drops lemon
5 drops black pepper
15 drops neroli
25 drops cedarwood
10 drops juniper
5 drops marjoram
5 drops clary sage
2 tbsp (25 ml) lavender flower water

Sweet and Gentle

This is a lovely, delicate, feminine cologne with hints of citrus and a honeyed sweet undertone. Particularly well suited to wear on days when you feel in need of some emotional support, this cologne surrounds you in a haze of comforting scent.

what's in it?
4 tbsp (50 ml) high proof vodka
20 drops linden blossom
10 drops bergamot
20 drops neroli
15 drops lavender
15 drops mandarin
5 drops jasmine
5 drops ambrette seed
10 drops rosewood
10 drops geranium
2 tbsp (25 ml) rose flower water

how're they made?

1 Fill a dark glass bottle (which can hold 4 fl oz [100 ml] of liquid) with the high proof vodka.

2 Carefully drop in the essential oils, one by one. Put on the bottle cap and shake vigorously for a few minutes to thoroughly dissolve the essential oils.

3 Top off with the flower water, and shake again. A small amount of essential oil may separate out and float on the top, so before using the cologne, remember to shake the bottle first each time.

4 Let the cologne stand for a week or two before using it. This allows the cologne to mature and the perfume to settle.

Manly Musk

This is another masculine fragrance with a distinctive musky note. Although musk itself is derived from animals, there are essential oils that give a musky fragrance. Nutmeg in particular is used in the perfume industry for its musklike aroma. Clove is another spice oil that has been used in perfumes extensively, and was one of the main ingredients used by the early Arab perfume makers.

what's in it?

4 tbsp (50 ml) high proof vodka

20 drops sandalwood

10 drops frankincense

20 drops nutmeg

15 drops clove

15 drops petitgrain

5 drops jasmine

10 drops vetiver

5 drops holy basil

10 drops clary sage

2 tbsp (25 ml) linden flower water

how's it made?

1 Fill a dark glass bottle (which can hold 4 fl oz [100 ml] of liquid) with the high proof vodka.

2 Carefully drop in the essential oils, one by one. Put on the bottle cap and shake vigorously for a few minutes to thoroughly dissolve the essential oils.

3 Top off with the flower water, and shake again. A small amount of essential oil may separate out and float on the top, so before using the cologne, remember to shake the bottle first each time.

4 Let the cologne stand for a week or two before using it. This allows the cologne to mature and the perfume to settle.

Did You Know? *Perfumes have not always been approved of. The Greek philosopher Plato considered perfumes immoral and likely to lead to licentious behavior.*

Tip: *Try carrying this body spray with you when you are traveling on a hot, sticky day. Remembering to shut your eyes first, spray the Summer Breezes over your face to cool down and refresh yourself.*

Body Sprays

How we apply perfume varies according to fashion. For instance, in ancient Rome, slave girls would dance with aromatic cones on their heads. The perfume was blended into a base of fat, so that when the girls became hot through dancing, the fat melted and the perfumed oil would drip down over their hair and bodies. In the modern world, perfumed body sprays are fashionable. These are dilute aromatic toilet waters that can be sprayed all over the body to give an overall fragrant effect. This provides an alternative to the more selective application of concentrated perfume to the pulse points behind the ears, inside of the wrists, and base of the throat.

The following body sprays are based on flower waters and essential oils that make natural plant-based perfume sprays. Many of the perfumed sprays commercially available are based on synthetic compounds and chemicals, which can cause allergies. These natural body sprays are much kinder to your skin and smell wonderful too.

Summer Breezes

On a hot summer's day, a cooling, perfumed body spray is a real treat to use. This perfume has hints of fresh mown hay and apples from the chamomile, together with green herbal and sweet floral notes. A tiny trace of citrus and spice gives the perfume a clean, sharp tang.

what's in it?

2 tsp (10 ml) high proof vodka
20 drops chamomile
10 drops linden blossom
10 drops geranium
10 drops clary sage
10 drops lavender
5 drops bergamot
5 drops coriander
5 drops neroli
6 tbsp (90 ml) rose water

how's it made?

1 Fill a 3 fl oz (100 ml) or 4 fl oz (125 ml) glass bottle—with a spray attachment—with the high proof vodka.

2 Carefully drop in the essential oils, one by one. Shake the bottle vigorously to dissolve the essential oils.

3 Top off with the rose water, and shake to mix thoroughly.

4 Let the perfume stand for a few days to settle and mature. Shake the bottle before using the perfume each time, as a few drops of essential oil may not be fully dissolved.

Lavender Calmer

Lavender is well loved for the calming effect it has on the emotions. Here it is blended with ylang ylang, which is deeply relaxing and sensuous, and neroli, which is a sweet smelling nerve tonic. Hints of citrus give a light top note to this sweet, floral calming perfume.

what's in it?
2 tsp (10 ml) high proof vodka

20 drops lavender

20 drops neroli

10 drops ylang ylang

10 drops lemon

5 drops bergamot

5 drops rosewood

5 drops palmarosa

6 tbsp (90 ml) cornflower water

how's it made?

1 Fill a 3 fl oz (100 ml) or 4 fl oz (125 ml) glass bottle—with a spray attachment—with the high proof vodka.

2 Carefully drop in the essential oils, one by one. Shake the bottle vigorously to dissolve the essential oils.

3 Top off with the cornflower water, and shake to mix thoroughly.

4 Let the perfume stand for a few days to settle and mature. Shake the bottle before using the perfume each time, as a few drops of essential oil may not be fully dissolved.

Did You Know? *The Lavender Calmer recipe uses cornflower water, which is one of the more unusual flower waters. It has a lovely, fresh, calming scent. However, if you don't have cornflower water, then this recipe is also good using rose or lavender flower waters instead.*

Did You Know? *Bergamot is a citrus fruit, closely related to the orange, and is generally regarded as the finest of the citrus fruits. Bergamot is featured in about forty percent of commercial perfumes.*

Orange Flower Blossom

This sweet, orange floral perfume reunites all the produce of the orange tree. Petitgrain is derived from the wood of the orange tree, orange is from the fruit, and neroli is from the orange flower blossom. The overall effect is a clean, sweet orange perfume that is full of laughter and smiles.

what's in it?

2 tsp (10 ml) high proof vodka
20 drops orange
20 drops neroli
20 drops petitgrain
10 drops bergamot
5 drops mandarin
6 tbsp (90 ml) orange flower water

how's it made?

1 Fill a 3 fl oz (100 ml) or 4 fl oz (125 ml) glass bottle—with a spray attachment—with the high proof vodka.

2 Carefully drop in the essential oils, one by one. Shake the bottle vigorously to dissolve the essential oils.

3 Top off with the orange flower water, and shake to mix thoroughly.

4 Let the perfume stand for a few days to settle and mature. Shake the bottle before using the perfume each time, as a few drops of essential oil may not be fully dissolved.

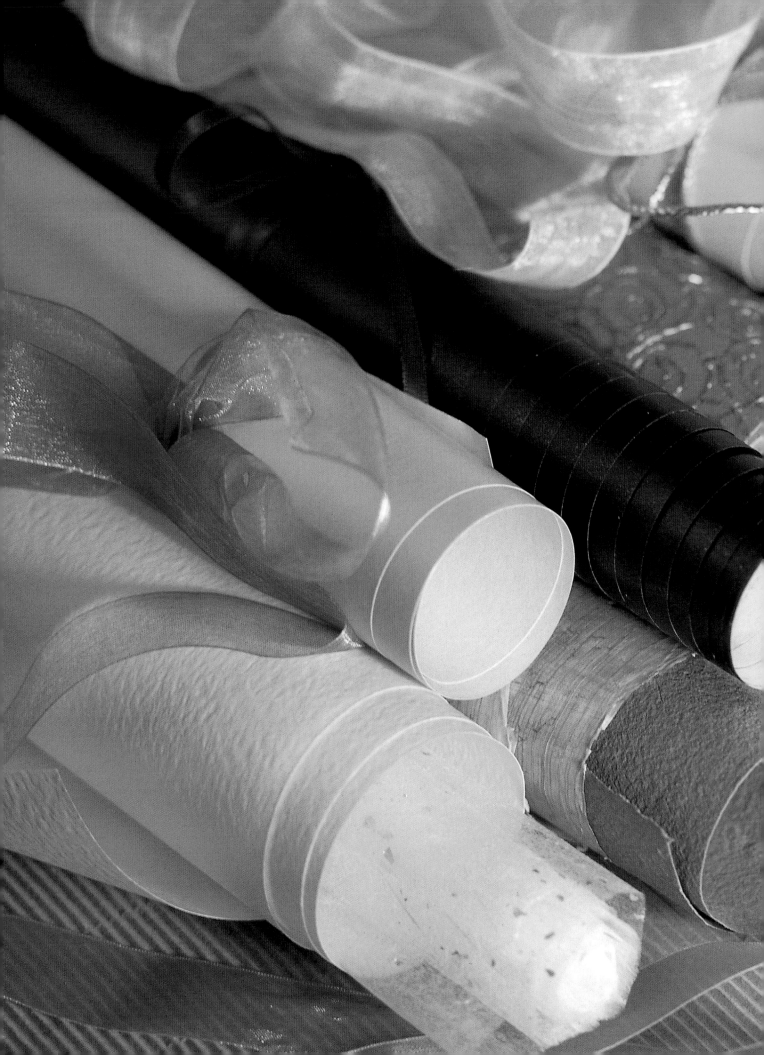

7 Gift Wrapping, Decorating, Boxing, and Displaying Soaps and Scents

Packaging and Decoration

Once you have made a batch or two of hand-crafted soap, it's time to think of how to package it. Because the soaps are natural, plant based, and use organic ingredients, it is appropriate for the packaging to reflect this. There are some beautiful natural packaging materials available. These include recycled corrugated cardboard, raffia, handmade papers, wicker baskets, and other natural packaging materials.

There are no hard and fast rules for packaging soaps, although using a breathable material is generally considered best for the soap. You can experiment with fabrics, dried banana leaves, and woods, as well as the materials mentioned above. Fragrant soaps made with essential oils should be wrapped as soon as possible after the curing process or drying time. The packaging acts a barrier against the air, so the scent is retained longer.

You may want to consider decorating your soaps before you package them. Although soaps made with spices, dried flowers, herbs, poppy seeds, or oats already have color and texture, you can add further detail. Plain soaps can be transformed by decoration. Some of the soap recipes suggest pushing a dried rosebud into the soap before it hardens. An alternative is to use melted paraffin wax—or candle wax—to affix a dried flower to the top of the soap after it has hardened. You could also affix an almond, vanilla pod, coffee bean, or section of cinnamon stick to indicate what ingredients went into the soap.

Another way to decorate your soap is to make an imprint. This should be done when the soap is firm, but not quite hard, in the middle of the curing or drying process. For an antique feel, use an old wax sealing stamp, the kind used to seal letters. You can find other stamps in kitchen stores among the cookie cutters and cake decorating utensils. These offer an imaginative alternative. Whatever implement you use, grease it first with a little vegetable oil so you make a clear, clean imprint, and so that it does not stick.

Scents are easier to pack than soaps, as they have already been made in or poured into a bottle. You can use ornamental glass bottles rather than plain glass bottles, so the perfumes are presented attractively. There is a wide range of ornamental glass bottles available, with etched glass, colored glass, stained glass, and decorated glass all having a different appeal. A range of bottles can be displayed on a dressing table or shelf for a dramatic effect.

If you are making a gift of a perfume bottle, then you can wrap the bottle in colored tissue paper to protect the fragile glass, and place this in a decorative box. Glass bottles are the traditional containers for scents, but if you want a historical feel, you can look for stone or porcelain bottles. These can make stunning gifts. Natural-colored sandstone bottles from India are particularly effective for a natural, organic look. Delicate porcelain bottles, sometimes available with spray attachments, offer a refined, sophisticated feel.

"The packaging material you select will depend on what look you want to give your soap."

–Catherine Bardey, *fashion stylist and author*

Tip: *Patterned translucent material or wrapping paper make particularly effective wrapping for glycerin soaps.*

Gift Wrapping

Wrapping your soaps in imaginative ways can make them look really professional and pretty. Here are some ideas for gift wrapping your soaps.

Choose a square of fabric according to what look you'd like to give the soap. Coarse, natural fabrics such as hessian or hemp give an organic feel and look, while silk and satin offer a more sophisticated look. Wrap the soap in the fabric just as you would a parcel. Tie a natural, organic cloth with raffia or brown string, and tie a silk or satin wrapped soap with a pretty ribbon.

Cut a strip of decorative or handmade paper that is half the length of the soap bar you want to wrap. Wrap round the middle of the soap so the two ends are exposed. To personalize the soap, affix a handmade label to the center of the decorative wrap. This can either describe the type of soap or it can be a personal design.

Make a drawstring pouch from natural or decorative fabric. Lace makes a particularly interesting pouch, and reveals the perfume and appearance of the soap. Create the drawstring by sewing a strip of fabric over a ribbon or cord at one end of the piece of fabric, leaving enough space so the cord can be drawn tight.

Wrap the soap bar in a simple square of plain white muslin. Choose some decorative dried flowers or herbs on stems that reflect the ingredients used in the soap. Use raffia or ribbon to tie a decorative bow around the muslin, and tie up the flower stems with the ribbon, so the flowers create an attractive bunch on the top of the wrapped soap.

You can make a strand of small soaps, wash balls, or bath bombs. Take a rectangular sheet of fabric and lay it on a flat surface. Allowing for a two inch (5 cm) border, place the individual soaps along the long edge of the fabric with a two inch (5 cm) space in between each soap. Carefully fold the fabric over the soaps and roll them up into a strand. Tie the ends and the spaces between the soaps with ribbon, string, or raffia. Finally, you can trim the ends of the fabric with pinking shears for added decorative effect.

Make a pretty lace effect with a paper doily. Place a bar of soap in the center, and gently gather up the edges to a bunch at the top. Tie up the bundle with a strip of lace. You can include the stems of a few dried rosebuds or other dried flowers in the lace, so the flower buds fall decoratively around the doily parcel.

Boxes and Ribbons

Once you've wrapped your soaps, you can pack them into boxes for a practical finishing touch. Although the soaps are quite hard, they can still be damaged even when wrapped. If you want to mail soaps as a gift to someone, putting them in a box first will protect them. However, the boxes can still be decorative and you can tie these with ribbons to make a beautiful gift. Here are some ideas for packing your soaps decoratively using boxes and ribbons.

As the quotation suggests, you can find small wooden crates and fill these with soaps. Try including both wrapped and unwrapped soaps nestled among shredded paper. You can make a bed of dried flowers and nestle a selection of unwrapped bars of soap for an organic look. For a more professional look, wrap soap bars in different colored tissue paper and alternate these in the crate. If the crate has slats, you can weave some raffia or ribbons in and out of the slats for added effect.

Natural, organic soaps can make a beautiful arrangement in a small wicker box or basket. Try placing dried baby pinecones and ornamental grasses in the bottom of a wicker basket and placing soap on the top. Wrap a sheet of cellophane around the arrangement, and glue the ends together underneath the basket. Take several strands of different colored raffia or ribbons and plait or weave them together, and then tie this over the top.

You can make a box using a sheet of corrugated cardboard. Place soap in the middle of a sheet of corrugated cardboard. With a sharp knife, gently score lines across the surface of the cardboard where you want to make the folds. The cardboard will then fold snugly to make a neat box. Take a long, wide velvet ribbon, and tie into a decorative bow. Carefully cut the long ends of the ribbon into strips, and tie a single rosebud at the end of half of the strips of ribbon for a stylish effect.

Take a cardboard box and half fill with potpourri. Place one or more soaps in among the potpourri and scatter more of the dried flowers and leaves on the top, so the soaps are half hidden. Seal the box, and tie a pretty ribbon around the box to

Tip: *A selection of scattered sea shells mingled amongst your soaps looks very attractive on a bathroom shelf.*

Displaying Your Soaps and Scents

Once you've made a range of soaps and scents, you will want to display all your hard efforts beautifully. In this way you can really appreciate how lovely your soaps and scents are. You've already read some ideas about how to decorate, wrap, and present your soaps and scents as gifts for others. Now you can try out some ideas on displaying soaps and scents in your home for yourself and your family.

Displaying your homemade scents is easy because they are already in pretty bottles, and look enchanting wherever you put them. One particularly attractive display is to line up a few bottles of your favorite scents in front of your dressing table mirror. The reflection of the bottles adds to the effect of the bottles themselves, and can make quite a dramatic sight.

Although your scent bottles should not be exposed to light, you can make an entrancing display by using empty scent bottles. You can also fill them with water to give the illusion of full scent bottles. Choose a small window with a window sill that has some direct sun for at least part of the day. Take a variety of crystals and attach fine silk or plastic thread to each one. Hang at different levels in the window, making sure a few hang right down to the window sill. Line up your bottles of scent among the hanging crystals. When the sun shines, you will have a magical scene of dancing reflections from the crystals and bottles.

Find a pretty soap dish to display your soaps on the bathroom basin and kitchen sink. You can also use other dishes and containers for a stunning effect. Try small white ceramic bowls, glass and stainless steel dishes, more often found among tableware. Japanese and Chinese stores have plenty of pretty ceramic dishes that can double up as attractive soap dishes.

For a really dramatic effect on the bathroom basin, use a thick slab of colored glass, or a trimmed piece of industrial metal. If you find a suitable but rough piece, most large hardware stores will be able to trim off any sharp edges for you. A tiny section of a wrought iron fence or gate makes an effective soap dish that also drains well.

A bathroom shelf, or freestanding bathroom unit, can take a display of soaps. In this way you can enjoy looking at them before you use them. They also give off a light delicate fragrance. Try making a tower of different soaps, with a couple of larger bars at the base, and building up to a small bar or wash ball on the top.

Handcrafted soaps mingled in with towels and linens on a bathroom shelf looks attractive, and the soaps also impart a hint of their fragrance to the linen. You can alternate along the shelf so you have a pile of towels next to a stack of soaps with perhaps a vase of dried flowers in the middle before another stack of soap and pile of towels.

8 Buying and Storing Fresh and Dried Ingredients

Tip: *Make sure you buy essential oil bottles that have a dropper insert. This allows you to count the number of drops accurately, so you end up with the correct amount.*

How to Buy and Store Ingredients

Buying and storing all your soap and perfume-making ingredients properly is fundamentally important to the overall process of making soaps and scents. The suppliers listed in the directory on pages 126–127 give you a range of suppliers of all the ingredients and equipment you will need to successfully make soaps and scents. Below are tips on buying and storing your ingredients properly, and also tips on storing your soaps and scents once you've made them.

- All ingredients are best bought fresh. Although the various ingredients for soaps and scents have differing shelf lives, it is a good habit to buy your ingredients only as you need them.

- Only buy sufficient quantities for your immediate requirements. Even though buying in bulk may be cheaper, unless you use it up quickly it could prove a false savings.

- Store your ingredients in a cool, dark, dry place away from drafts, light, damp, and heat. This will help prolong shelf life.

- Make sure you store your bottles of essential oils upright, in a cool dark place.

- Fresh ingredients such as fruits should be as fresh as possible, especially organic produce.

- If you have used half a bag of soap flakes, laundry starch, or similar dry product, make sure you reseal the bag well and remove all air. Or you could transfer the remainder into a airtight plastic container.

- Color bases of ground spices in oil will keep for a couple of months in an airtight, dark glass jar.

- If you think something has spoiled because it has discolored or changed texture, throw it away and buy new supplies. Using old ingredients could affect how a recipe turns out, and you don't want to waste other ingredients.

- Handcrafted soaps will last between six months and a year if you store them away from dust and excess light once they have fully dried out or cured. A helpful tip is to give away extra soaps as you make them, so you are not left with a cupboard full.

- Homemade scents based on oil will last up to six months. Scents based on alcohol will last a lot longer, as alcohol is a natural preservative. Scents based on flower waters are best used up within three months.

Troubleshooting

Here are some of the common problems that arise from cold-process soap making, together with a few hints on how to avoid them.

Tracing does not occur

Tracing can require a lot of patience, as it may still happen well after the time it's supposed to. Don't give up until you are quite sure the mixture is not going to trace, or after twenty-four hours. The probable reasons why tracing did not occur are: too much water or not enough lye, temperature was too high or too low, stirring the mixture ineffectually or too slowly. Next time ensure you measure all ingredients accurately and the temperature of fats and lye precisely.

The soap mixture is grainy

This is an aesthetic problem only, and the soap is safe to use. Grainy soap is caused by too high or too low temperatures, or by not stirring briskly or regularly enough.

The soap is soft and spongy

It is unlikely these bars will harden enough to use, so throw them away. Soft soap is caused by not using enough lye.

The soap is hard and brittle

You must throw these bars away as they are too alkaline for the skin. Hard soap is caused by using too much lye.

Air bubbles in the soap

Check that the bubbles only contain air. If there is liquid in the bubbles, you will have to throw the soap away, because the liquid will be mostly lye. If the bubbles are only air, the soap is fine to use. Air bubbles are caused by stirring too briskly (whipping or beating the mixture) or stirring for too long before pouring into the mold.

The soap mixture separates

Here you end up with a layer of hard soap underneath an oily liquid top layer. This soap must be thrown away. Separation is caused by insufficient stirring, too much lye, being poured into the mold too soon, or once poured the soap cooled too quickly.

Soap is marbled with white streaks

Make sure there are no chunks of slippery, solid lye. If they are just streaks then the soap is fine to use. Streaking is caused by uneven stirring, the temperature at which the lye and fats were mixed was too cold, or the soap was stirred for too long after adding the essential oils.

Curdling

The soap looks a bit like cottage cheese, or has small, pearly lumps forming at the bottom of the pan. The soap should be thrown away. Curdling is caused by inaccurate measurements or incorrect temperatures, irregular stirring, or cooling too quickly.

Soap has hard white chunks after hardening

Throw this soap away as the chunks are lye and the soap is too caustic to use. This is caused by using too much lye or stirring was too slow or ineffective.

Excessive soda ash on top of the cured soap

A small amount of soda ash is expected from the curing process. This is harmless and can easily be trimmed off. If, however, there is a lot and you have to cut deep into the soap to remove it, then the soap is too alkaline and must be thrown away. Excessive soda ash is caused by using too much lye.

Tip: *Take careful, detailed notes each time you make soap, including descriptions of each stage of the soap making. If something isn't quite perfect the first time, then you can make minor adjustments to quantities and procedures to improve things next time around.*

Glossary of Ingredients

Almond Oil (More precisely, sweet almond oil)
A base oil and a nutrient that can be used in all different types of soap. Ideal as a base oil for roll-on perfumes.

Avocado Oil
A nutrient oil high in vitamins A, D, E, and fatty acids. Has healing properties and is easily absorbed by the skin. Used to add moisturizing qualities to soaps.

Block Glycerin
Used to make glycerin soaps.

Caustic Soda
Also known as lye when in solution. Caustic soda's chemical name is sodium hydroxide. It is the alkaline or base used in cold-process soap making.

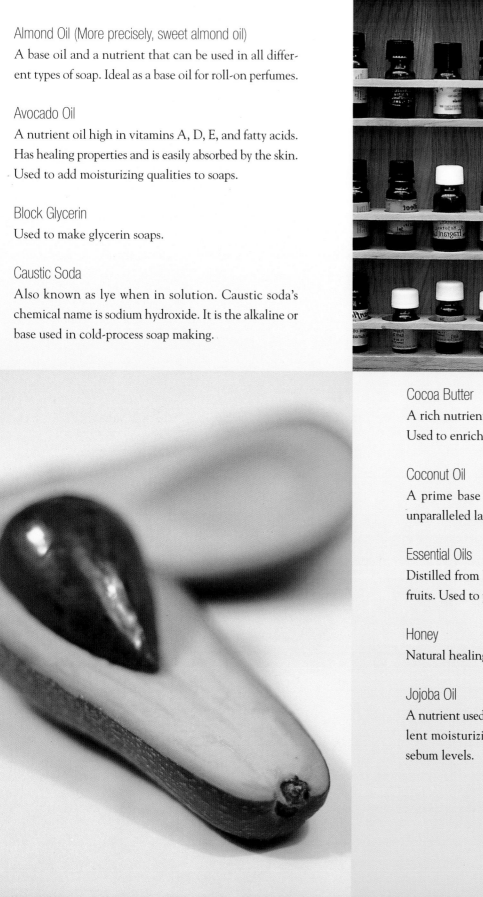

Cocoa Butter
A rich nutrient good for softening and protecting skin. Used to enrich soaps and give moisturizing qualities.

Coconut Oil
A prime base oil in cold-process soap making with unparalleled lathering and moisturizing properties.

Essential Oils
Distilled from herbs, flowers, woods, resins, and citrus fruits. Used to perfume soaps and scents.

Honey
Natural healing nutrient used to enrich soaps.

Jojoba Oil
A nutrient used in soap; actually a liquid wax. Has excellent moisturizing qualities. Helps skin retain normal sebum levels.

Kukui Nut Oil

An excellent moisturizing nutrient used in soaps. Has been shown to help heal skin conditions such as acne, eczema, psoriasis, and sunburned skin.

Liquid Glycerin

A syrupy, clear liquid that is good for moisturizing and healing dry skin. A nutrient used in soap.

Monoi de Tahiti

A soft, waxy block made from coconut oil and perfumed with gardenia flowers. Used to enrich and perfume soaps.

Olive Oil

Light olive oil has excellent moisturizing qualities and is very mild. It has poor lathering qualities, so is best used in conjunction with other base oils in cold-process soap making

Rosehip Granules

Ground dried rosehips. Gives a pinky-peach color to soaps and gives a slightly grainy texture.

Rosehip Oil

The best available is Rosa Mosquetta. It is high in essential fatty acids and gamma linolenic acid, and helps regenerate the skin. A healing nutrient used to enrich soaps.

Shea Butter

Also known as Karite nut butter. Excellent skin moisturizing qualities; especially healing for dry, damaged, and irritated skin. A valuable nutrient in soap making.

Soya Bean Oil

A base oil for cold-process soap making. Contributes bulk, mildness, and a stable lather. Best used in combination with other oils and nutrients that have good skin moisturizing qualities.

Spices and Herbs

Ground spices and herbs are used to color soaps naturally. They include alkanet root, turmeric, cinnamon, and paprika.

Directory of Suppliers in the USA and UK

Suppliers in the USA

Angel's Earth
1633 Scheffer Avenue
St Paul, MN 55116
Tel: (612) 698-3636

Aquarius Aromatherapy & Soap
PO Box 2971
Sumas, WA 98295-2971
Tel: (604) 826-4199
adriana@aquariusaroma-soap.com

Essential Oil Company
1719 Southeast Umatilla Street
Portland, OR 97202
Tel: (800) 729-5912
order@essentialoil.com

Pourette
6910 Roosevelt Way Northeast
Seattle, WA 98115
Tel: (206) 525-4488

Prima Fleur Botanicals Inc
12,01-R Andersen Drive
San Rafael, CA 94901
Tel: (415) 455-0957

Sunfeather Handcrafted Herbal Soap Company
1551 Highway 72
Potsdam, NY 13676
Tel: (206) 525-4488 or (315) 265-3648

Suppliers in the UK

Ascent Pure Fragrance Natural Perfumery
Long Barn
Felindre
Brecon
Powys LD3 0TE
Tel: (01497) 847788
morrisj@gonegardening.com

G Baldwin & Co
173 Walworth Road
London SE17 1RW
Tel: (020) 7252 6264
sales@baldwins.co.uk

Essentially Oils
8-10 Mount Farm
Junction Road
Churchill
Chipping Norton
Oxfordshire OX7 6NP
Tel: (01608) 659544
sales@essentiallyoils.com

Fragrant Earth Co Ltd
Orchard Court
Magdalene Street
Glastonbury
Somerset BA6 9 EW
Tel: (01458) 831 361
all-enquiries@fragrant-earth.com

Nature's Treasures
Bridge Industrial Estate
New Portreath Road
Bridge
Near Redruth
Cornwall TR16 4QL
Tel: (01209) 843881
naturestreasures@ndirect.co.uk

Acknowledgments

I would like to thank Robin Bath, Toby Matthews, Angie Patchell, and Winnie Prentiss for their talented assistance in bringing this book to fruition.

I would also like to thank my partner, Robert Beer, for his loving support throughout the writing of this book, and for willingly trying out different soaps.

Nicki at Woodspirits UK provided valuable tips and support during my soap making, and supplied a few additional soaps for the photographs in this book. Nicki offers a range of beautiful handcrafted soaps, and can be contacted at:

Woodspirits UK, Unit 42, New Lydenburg Industrial Estate, New Lyndenburg Street London SE7 8NE. Tel/Fax: (020) 8293 4949. Email: woodspiritsuk@compuserve.com.

I would also like to thank the following businesses for the kind provision of materials for the photography:

4 my way of life, 13–15 Jerdan Place, Fulham, London SW6 1BE
The Chelsea Gardener, 125 Sydney Street, London SW3 6NR
Cologne & Cotton Ltd., 791 Fulham Road, London SW6 5HD
Damask, 3–4 Broxholme House, New Kings Road, London SW6 4AA
Paperchase, 213 Tottenham Court Road, London, W1T 7PS
pH Factor, 183 New Kings Road, London SW6 4SW
toute-bagai, 160 Wandsworth Bridge Road, London SW6 2UH
Sasha Waddell, 269 Wandsworth Bridge Road, London SW6 2TX
Sue Walker, 166 Wandsworth Bridge Road, London SW6 2UH